The Magic Apple Tree
A Country Year

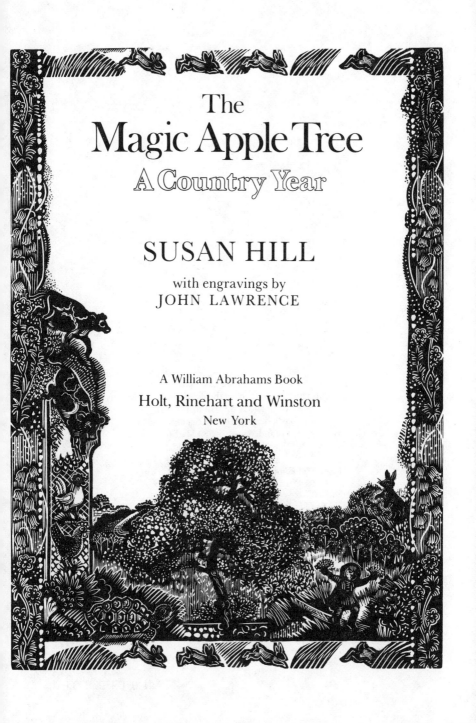

The
Magic Apple Tree
A Country Year

SUSAN HILL

with engravings by
JOHN LAWRENCE

A William Abrahams Book
Holt, Rinehart and Winston
New York

First published in the United States in 1983 by
Holt, Rinehart and Winston, 383 Madison Avenue,
New York, New York 10017.

Library of Congress Cataloging in Publication Data
Hill, Susan, 1942–
The magic apple tree.
1. Barley (Oxfordshire)—Social life and customs.
2. Country life—England—Barley (Oxfordshire)   3. Hill,
Susan, 1942–   I. Title.
DA690.B2293H54 1983   942.5'71   83-8450
ISBN 0-03-063399-0

First American Edition

Printed in the United States of America
1 3 5 7 9 10 8 6 4 2

ISBN 0-03-063399-0

For
Stanley and Jessica
With love

CONTENTS

THE MAGIC apple tree is bare now. Stand at the top of the seven stone steps. Moon Cottage, and that part of the garden that lies in front of it, are at your feet, and the apple tree is straight ahead, your eyes are level with its lower branches. Through them, you see the rise and fall of the fields beyond, piled upon one another like pillows. The Buttercup field, which is nearest, slopes down to the small brook that runs between four willows; beyond that, the Rise, overlapping with the Dovehouse field, and so gently on, and up, to where the topmost field lies like an arm outstretched, and forms a boundary to one side of the village. On a few, very clear days in winter, you can even see further, right over the top of the apple tree to where the blue hump of the village of Hope – Hope-on-the-Slope – is sometimes visible. But, mostly, there is mist or some other greyness obscuring it, and later in the year it is almost blocked out by the foliage.

The fields within a few acres of this house, the fields you can see through the branches of the apple tree, are all small, and in winter they are empty; these are long-established grazing fields for cattle and horses, never ploughed or planted. They are bounded by hedges of hawthorn and elder, knotted with groups of trees that thicken as the ground rises in the distance, the trees of light, mixed woodlands, sycamore and ash, birch and maple, mingling with all the smaller trees of the village gardens, laburnum and rowan, cherry, plum and pear. But, now, you can identify them only by their outlines. Through them all, and through the magic apple tree, we can see the roofs and walls, gates and fences, of the houses on the east side of the village, the slope which rises above Fen Lane, and those down in its groin; and, after dark, we see their lights. Once their leaves are full again, they too will be concealed and we will feel more isolated. It is a comfort in winter to see those signs of life on the long nights of early dark, we feel drawn towards them. When the leaves shut us off from one another again, and the lights are not lit until nine or ten o'clock, there is warmth outdoors, and light in the sky itself, and then people go for evening walks and meet in the lanes, stand to talk at gates, look over into one another's gardens. But in winter, when we all scurry back into our individual burrows, and no one lingers, we need to be able to see each other's houses and lights, for reassurance.

Whether you stand at the top of the stone steps or at any of the windows, you cannot look from this cottage across to the fields opposite, or to your left, away and down over the whole, flat stretch of the Fen, without also having the apple tree in your sight, it draws your eyes towards it and balances the picture, a point of reference for the whole view. It is only, perhaps, fifteen feet high, and a most beautiful, satisfying shape, it has the dome, falling down to a wider base frill, of the shaggy parasol mushroom. Samuel Palmer could have painted it, this is the shape of so many of his trees in the pictures of the fields and gardens around Shoreham. It is what I first saw when I opened the gate and stood at the top of the stone steps, the day I found Moon Cottage. At once, I thought of Palmer, who has always been close to my heart; it felt like a sign on that day and it does so still, the spirit of the place is in that apple tree.

It is very old, and the tips of the branches are brittle in winter; when the sap is dry, you can snap them off with scarcely any pressure. The trunk is knobbly and each branch and twig twists and turns back upon itself, like old, arthritic hands.

On winter nights, small owls perch there, to scan the immediate fields, for it is a perfect look-out point. If you stand very still and in darkness at one of the upstairs windows, you are on the owl's level, if it turns its head, you may catch a glimpse of the hooded eyes. Stay long enough, and you will see it take off, suddenly, silently, from the tree, and skim down fast on to some creature lying in the under-growth.

We have hung an old, weatherbeaten feeding tray from one of its lower branches, so that in the daylight hours of the winter the whole tree seethes with small birds, hopping and bobbing; tits, finches, sparrows, the robin, go constantly to and fro for nuts and scraps and seeds, the old stone flags at the foot of the tree are spattered with their droppings.

There is always a wind about here, we are so exposed on all sides, and in late autumn and winter the apple tree stands up to the gales which hurl across the Fen and up the slope towards us, with nothing until they reach it, above its stone wall, to break their force. There have been terrible nights when I have lain awake listening to the roar and boom, hearing branches groan and break, stakes and fences come up out of the ground like pulled teeth, slates and tiles slip and smash down, and I have feared for our frail-seeming tree, and in the mornings have gone out to survey the debris of the night and been afraid to look in its direction. One February night, a single blast of wind, the eye of the storm, took half our heavy, wooden fence, the glass roof of a neighbour's greenhouse, a lilac bush beyond it, two chimney pots and an open garage door, it simply gathered them up into itself and flung them down again some yards away. But the apple tree still stood, resilient, indomitable as some small wooden ship on a stormy sea. After that, I did not worry about it.

On clear winter nights, I go outside and stand underneath it, look up. Through the bare, down-curving branches, I see the moon, ringed with frost, and the hard, bright points of stars in a cold sky. The apple tree contains them within its shape and forms a shelter over me, it gives a framework to this place, the cottage, the garden, the near countryside, and to my vision of them. I should not like to lose it.

The Village in Winter

APART FROM a short, hard frost over Christmas, it had so far been a wet winter, mild and dank, 'a green winter', a winter of those fogs and mists that hang over all the ditches and dykes of the Fen. Barley is set on a hill and runs away in a horse-shoe shape down two sides of it, two hundred feet above the Fen, and all the water runs down there, too, for the land just beneath your feet, wherever you stand, is a mesh of small streams, the veins of the village. So when it rains, as it had so far this winter, Barley is soon dry again but the Fen is a bog, often flooded for weeks at a time, in spite of new and supposedly improved drainage systems, installed by farmers down there in the hopes of making some of the land more suitable for corn.

November, December, January. From Moon Cottage we looked down on those flat, water-filled fields, water that gleams the colour of gunmetal, with a grey sky above. It sounds drear and drear it can be, lowering to the spirits of the watcher, day after day. Yet it is also strangely beautiful, in the sombre way of those Dutch or Norwich landscape painters whose glories lie in the greyness of sky and wind-torn clouds, and in every subtle variation in the way the winter light is reflected down on to the wet fields and back again. The views from Moon Cottage, and from all of Barley in winter, are like those paintings, one third land, and two thirds sky.

For weeks, the daylight never seemed to come up fully, it was still dark after eight o'clock in the morning, and again by three, lamps were kept on all day. And so, because of the wet, low Fen and the mild days, followed sometimes by intensely cold nights, there were those mysterious mists, when the stumps of posts and hedges and the blackened upper branches of trees reared up out of the coiling whiteness, their trunks and the ground on which they stood remaining shrouded. On those days, I can well believe all the ghost stories of the Fen; there were riots among the cottagers and farm-labourers who lived below Barley centuries ago, after the Enclosure of what were their Common Lands, and the troublemakers were, it was said, sometimes put to death in secret, and have returned to haunt the places ever since. And then there is the story of the man murdered in a hayrick, a pitchfork plunged through his heart and mysterious marks burnt into the ground below, the marks of witchcraft.

Even on these raw, wet days, I like to go for a walk through the village, and down on to the Fen itself, for the pleasure of doing so, seeing what looks different, who is about, and to stretch my legs after a morning at my desk. But, when the mist hangs about down there, I am uneasy once I have passed the last house down the lane and am walking alone between the dripping hedgerows. There is no traffic, these lanes that lead down from Barley are all dead ends, and there seem to be no creatures, either, except for a donkey standing like a stone in a field full of mist and thistles; the farm animals are housed in their barns for the winter, the birds are silent and invisible, apart from the occasional crow flying low, a dark shadow over the sodden land.

On the Fen it is quiet and the air seems muffled, pressing in around me, the mist drifts into my hair and clings to my face, I feel stifled by it and I can see only a yard or two ahead. I turn my back and walk faster up the slope again, where the air is at once fresher. I see no one at all. I am anxious to be home. This is the most alienating and unsociable of all weathers in the country. No one goes outside unless they must, and then, like me, they walk fast, heads down, on their way to the letter-box; there is nothing to be done on the sodden ground of the garden and the farm-land is waterlogged too. That is one of the great differences between life in the village and in the town, especially in winter which, after all, lasts for more than half the year, and it has driven away many who are not naturally withdrawn, cannot take the solitude and the emptiness of fields and lanes, the apparent monotony. In the town, bad weather is unpleasant, but it does not have such a drastic, tangible effect on everyday social life. People congregate at the shops, and walk dogs and prams, ride their bicycles down the streets, they brave rain and gales and early dark going to and from their places of work and the stations and car parks, libraries and markets, there is always someone to be seen from the windows. When we lived in the city and Jessica was a baby, I pushed her out whatever the weather and the suburban avenues were always full of people. We did not know many of them, but there was usually someone to nod to and complain to about the weather. But country lanes in winter are different, they are lonely places. I do not mind that in the least, and besides, there is a hidden social life behind the doors and drawn curtains of villages all winter through, the appearance of emptiness and silence, lack of life, is deceptive. Nevertheless, I can understand that the solitude, the dankness and early dark, the absence of human activity, immediately beyond the window, oppresses some and can make the everyday business of country life lonely and wearisome.

For all that Barley lies in a comparatively mild inland county and for all that much of the winter is often greyness, fog and damp, there are bouts of severe weather and then, because we stand on a hill, and all the approaches to us are uphill ones, and because we are, so to speak, a dead end, on the road to no other village or town, we are very easily cut off here, and very exposed to blizzard and bitter winds that drive the snow before them to block off the lanes.

It was on the second Tuesday in January – W.I. night – that last winter became a serious and dramatic matter, a cold, tiring, but exhilarating time, at least for the young, and a companionable time for all, when we were stranded, snowbound and sealed off in place and, it seemed, in time too, for the usual pattern of the day's coming and going was halted.

We had been in the town all day, and I had scarcely noticed the weather. But, by the time I put the car up the last, steep bit of hill, past Cuckoo Farm and Foxley Spinney, towards the village, the sky had gathered like a boil, and had an odd, sulphurous yellow gleam over iron grey. It was achingly cold, the wind coming north-east off the Fen made us cry. We ran down the steps and indoors, switched on the lamps and opened up the stove, made tea, shut out the weather, though we could still hear it, the wind made a thin, steely noise under doors and through all the cracks and crevices of the old house. But by six o'clock there had been one of those sudden changes. I opened the door to let in Hastings, the tabby cat, and sensed it at once. The wind had dropped and died, everything was still and dark as coal, no moonlight, not a star showed through the cloud cover, and it was just a degree warmer. I could smell the approaching snow. Everything waited.

Another hour later, setting off for the W.I., I saw the first, fat flakes as they came softly down and settled at once as they touched the ground. I bent and touched them. They were oddly dry, grainy. They would last. I put on my coat and boots and took the lantern.

The W.I. hall, which was the village school a hundred years ago, stands in the lee of the church of St. Nicholas at the top of the lane that leads from Moon Cottage. It is stone-built, barn-shaped, with high windows and poor lighting, and the walls are curiously adorned with sporting trophies, the antlered heads of long-dead stags, and glass cases full of stuffed fox, fish and stoat.

There are no street lamps in Barley and on a dark night like this you cannot see further than the end of your nose. But ahead, up the lane, I could see other lanterns and torches bobbing on, as the ladies made their way up to the hall. In the doorway, we tested the temperature of the building and kept on our coats and scarves and boots. People coming in cars from outlying farms, or the next village, which does not have an Institute, spoke uneasily of the bad weather forecast and the need to get away early; snow powdered hats and coat-shoulders and was filling up the ruts in the cart track outside, softly, steadily.

Our domestic business was hurried through. The speaker for the evening, who had come twelve miles to tell us about her travels in

9

Arabia (at the age of seventy!), was in a direct line from those intrepid female adventurers of the nineteenth century who crossed mountain ranges by mule with only native scouts for company, and ventured into remote and dangerous areas of the desert in search of early pottery fragments. Her talk was later described in the minutes as 'fascinating' but she gave it at top speed and omitted the showing of her slides altogether, so nervous was she about being marooned in Barley by the bad weather. By nine o'clock we had disbanded and the snow was inches deep and still falling like goose feathers. It was a convivial, even giggly walk down the dark lane, with elderly ladies clutching one another's arms, torches dropped and extinguished at once, buried in the snow, and a certain air of excitement, for all the complaining.

At five in the morning, I woke to a wonderful silence. I went to the window and pushed it open carefully. A little heap of snow fell inwards on to the ledge. A light wind was taking it now, and moulding and shaping it against the hedges and fences. Everything was bone-white, under the riding moon. I wanted to go out and walk in the fields by myself, to watch for owls and foxes and smell the night smells. Dull common sense and tiredness prevailed. I returned to bed and have ever afterwards regretted it, for such times come rarely and the countryside under the first, heavy fall of snow at four in the morning is a changed and an enchanted place, the imagination would feed upon the memory of it for ever after.

Next morning, the snow had turned pink, and the sky was pink, too, the whole Fen and all the snow-covered fields between seemed to glow with it, as the sun rose. Then the light changed as it climbed higher, and on the near horizon we could see more snow clouds, banked one upon the other, menacing, moving nearer. I felt excited, babbled of sledges and skis, snowmen and snowballs. Intending to go up the stone steps as usual to collect mail and milk and newspaper from the box in the wall, I opened the front door and stepped out and up to my knees in snow. The steps were not to be seen, and the stone wall dividing us from the Buttercup field, below the apple tree, was concealed too, under the hummocks and billows of wind-blown snow. It was clear that there would have been no deliveries.

After half an hour or so of hard digging, scraping and shoving back, we carved a narrow path out to the lane, but no further. Moon Cottage was cut off from Geranium Cottage, belonging to our neighbour Mr Elder, and from Fen Cottage opposite, and School Lane was cut off from the rest of the village, and the village from the world. Across the snow, we saw other people with shovels and waved to them, stranded on our island. I wondered about old Miss Reevers, alone in the very last cottage, before the lane peters out into the fields, and how much food we had and how long it would be before Stanley would get to work again.

But I spent my childhood in North Yorkshire, long hard winters were usual; buses could not run and we walked to school through snowdrifts; farms and villages were cut off for weeks on end. None of that would happen in Barley, yet I felt, at least on this first morning, the old, childish excitement.

Extremes of bad weather and being isolated by them does bring out the best in village communities and shows up all the strengths of this way of life. There are about five hundred souls in Barley, and more than half of them are over sixty, quite a few well over eighty. It is a companionable village, and fairly compact but, because of its situation, set on a hill, it is badly placed for vehicles to negotiate the lanes in snow and ice. It was only two and a half days before the ploughs got to us, fast followed by the delivery vans, and before we ourselves could, albeit hazardously, get out, but I have not enjoyed a time so well for years, or felt so at one with my neighbours, so useful and purposeful, touched by that spirit of blitz and blizzard which my generation, and those after it, has lacked much experience of. This may seem a sentimental view. It is not. Of course, we were not suffering any extremes of deprivation, we had electricity and water and food, no one was taken seriously ill, we telephoned each other with offers and requests, we could walk about. In the West country, where many villages were inaccessible for weeks, an emergency local radio station was set up to broadcast news and weather information, and it knitted local communities together, over the air if not in the flesh, it cheered, informed and alerted. We had no need of such a measure, but if we had been in severe difficulty, we could have got by, with a sense of solidarity. The young and strong trudged through the snow to share supplies and take messages, the housebound and elderly made hot drinks and received more visitors in those few days than often during weeks of normal life. Meals-on-wheels became meals-on-foot, the village school remained closed, but for once the pub was entirely full of locals only, and its car park was empty.

And oh, the joy for the children, to live within reach of so many sloping, snow-covered fields. All day they slid and tobogganed, ran and tumbled and pelted one another; standing at the window, I looked down on such scenes as Brueghel created, and at the end of the afternoons the lanes were lined with coloured gnome-figures in woollen hats, the little ones half asleep, pulled on sledges or carried on shoulders, noses red as berries, hands raw as meat, voices hoarse with shouting. It was the most carefree, joyous of interludes, the world was as far off as the moon, and just as unreal, its doings could not touch us. I wanted it never to end.

But, waking at dawn on Saturday, I heard the slip and slide and bump of loosening snow, the patter of rain on the windows. The sky was the colour of a gull's back and the snow just a little darker, already smirched and soiled-looking.

The thaw had begun.

Moon Cottage

THOSE TIMES of my life when I have been entirely at peace with myself and in tune with the world, when I have felt happy and relaxed, satisfied and light of heart, have all been spent either by the sea, or in the country.

All through my thirties, since marriage and, most particularly, since the birth of my daughter, I experienced a growing discontent and dissatisfaction with town life. I seemed to be only skimming the surface of things, to be cramped and hurried and tense, I noticed the smell and noise of the traffic more, and I worried above all about the influences of the city upon Jessica, of so much that was ugly and tawdry and meretricious, violent, distasteful, of all the getting and spending. I longed for more space around me, for growing things and time and all the sounds and scents of the natural world on my doorstep, for peace and quiet in which to do my own work, and to provide a counterbalance for Jessica to the time she would inevitably have to spend in the city. I wanted to give her a rich treasure-store of country memories, sights and smells, sounds and colours, on which she could draw for the rest of her life. A friend of mine, who has lived in a north of England city for forty years, feeds off a memory of running through fields, up to her waist in buttercups, on a day's outing to the country when she was six years old. A very old, and wise friend said, 'There are so many *good* things for a child to do in the country.' Oh yes, and not just a child, either.

We endured the ribaldry. 'Back to nature?' and 'What price the rural idyll?' or, if they were sentimental, 'Ah, an old stone cottage with roses round the door!' But we were clear-eyed and realistic about how our everyday life was likely to be, and knew we would have to compromise, at least for the time being, with the demands of work and school, and not isolate ourselves too far from the city. We nurtured no dreams of self-sufficiency, nor of those roses round the door. If we had had those, I would not have driven out to Barley on a lowering, drizzling afternoon at the back end of November, when 'beeches dripped in browns and duns' and the village street was entirely deserted. Moon Cottage, in spite of the magic apple tree, looked neglected, cold, dull. It is not, even in the softest of summer sunshine, a beautiful house. It was once three poky labourers' cottages, built of that mottled Oxfordshire limestone, and once thatched, but now ordinarily tiled. It lies at right angles to the lane, facing uncompromisingly north.

It had been empty for a year and casually tenanted for a further year prior to that. The garden, which lies on three sides, was rank and overgrown, dead hollyhock stalks poked up like bones from the shrivelled nettles and couch grass, slime spread over the paths, and when I went inside, the cold came off the walls, and rose from the floor, a damp, seeping cold that smelled fungoid, sweetish and unpleasant. The sloping roof over the storehouse sagged in the middle like an old bed, there were mice droppings and an eerie grey mould growing out of some of the cracks in the bathroom, the beams in the kitchen had been painted bright blue and the sitting-room was lit by wall-lamps that dripped plastic candle-grease; most carefully placed in the centre of the large window overlooking the finest view was a Dickensian-style bottle-glass pane.

We would have to stretch our financial resources to afford the basic asking price, and I did rough mental arithmetic to assess the cost of the work that would obviously have to be done to make the cottage mortgageable and habitable. We could not sensibly afford it.

But Barley was the right village, I knew that. It is only six miles from the city, and feels a hundred and six, it is so peaceful, so thoroughly rural are its surroundings. There is no through traffic, it is well-shaped and has so many superb views, the houses are modest and pleasing, the size of the place is right, large enough to have some community life and yet not too large. And we would be hard put to it to find anything so perfectly situated as Moon Cottage, open to the countryside for miles around.

I went outside again. It was absolutely quiet. I looked up at the walls and found a stone above the kitchen window carved with the date, 1742, bang in the middle of the period when most of the cottages here were built; and an old fire insurance plaque with Britannia just discernible through the mildew. I went back in. There were two staircases, one on either side of the house, and endless nooks and crannies, oddly-shaped cupboards, sloping ceilings. I liked the way the stairs seemed to have been built vertically, rather than on a slant, and to incorporate a vicious curve half-way up. From every half-landing and landing you could see the countryside, the magic apple tree and then miles of field and Fen beyond. I imagined how it would be when the sky was clear and the light brighter. The main bedroom had no straight lines in it at all, ceiling and walls wandered vaguely, sloped and met again. There was a small window-door. I stepped out and on to the roof, and felt as if I were on battlements, I was looking right into the topmost branches of the apple tree.

The window on the other side of the room faced the village, a less bleak, more companionable view. I saw thatched and slated roofs, stone walls, an old-fashioned greenhouse, the church tower, with its clock.

I do not like dark houses and so many cottages we had looked at were dark and claustrophobic – as was, after all, traditional; or else, worse, they had been opened out to the daylight by metal-framed slabs of picture-window, which I hate because they are so unfitted to the style of the English country cottage. But Moon Cottage had exactly the right lightness and sense of space, though it is not really very big, every room upstairs had two windows, one on each side, though they were wooden-framed and cross-paned, the right sort of windows. And, even on such a dull day, so much light came from so much sky on three sides, yet the cottage was sheltered, set below the level of the lane on the fourth.

I could say that I knew we would live here the moment I saw it, because it was, in all essentials, what we had been looking for, the right house in the right place, and that would be true; and because of the signals it gave out, the spirit I responded to, and because of the apple tree. But there was one thing more. If no one else believes, let alone understands it, it does not matter, it is enough that it happened, and *I* know it. When I saw Moon Cottage, I recognised it at once, and as I had driven up to Barley, I knew that I would, because I had dreamed about it.

A few weeks earlier, one bitterly cold Sunday, we had come to Barley for the first time in our lives to have lunch with an old friend. Her cottage is tiny and set under a thick, beetling thatch, at the top of the lane opposite the church. When we arrived we looked quickly about us but it was not a day for lingering in the wind. In any case, you can't see Moon Cottage from there, it is hidden round the bend, and down in its own hollow at the foot of the stone steps.

Jane has a rather enclosed garden, though because it was November, we caught a glimpse of her view towards the Fen. It was not looking its best, or most interesting, the winter light was not, as it sometimes is, slanting and mysterious, merely flat, but I could not take my eyes off it, and even though I had seen precious little of the village itself, it all felt right, and I began asking questions about living here. The family probably thought I was mad. And, by the time we started for home, it was almost dark and sleeting hard, the wind came howling up the lane into our faces. Not a roses-round-the-door-day, no.

That night, I dreamed a dream in which I stood in the garden of a cottage further down the lane, at Barley, under an apple tree, looking out over the Fen. I could see much more of it now. Then, I turned and went inside, and closed the door.

When I woke, I knew, I knew absolutely certainly that the cottage existed, that when I saw it I should recognise it, and that we would live there. The following morning, Jane telephoned. If I had meant what I said about the possibility of coming to Barley, there was a cottage, further down the lane. It was empty, was thought to have been sold, but the deal had just fallen through. Moon Cottage was on the market again.

My inner certainty that followed upon the dream never left me, though, like a candle light, it flickered and all but went out, during the following six months, and all the complications, anxieties and pendulum swings of house selling and buying, for I did not see how it could possibly come about, all seemed set against us, Moon Cottage could never be ours.

A year later, when another November gale was beating at the doors and windows, I paused in the middle of weighing out currants and sultanas for the Christmas cake, and remembered the dream, and the telephone call from Jane, the day I came here, and I put aside my baking things and went all around the house, seeing it as ours now, noting how much we had done, all the marks of our family life, sensing the roots we had already put down.

There had been no drastic alterations, though a lot of work and money went into righting the concealed defects of damp, draught and decay, into re-wiring and plumbing and re-flooring. But I believe you need to handle an old house carefully, restrain the first urge to knock down and replace and add on, or even to restore; you need to settle to a place, give it time to speak to you, about itself, rub along with things as they are and see how they work. There has been so much lost, so much alteration and modernisation and ruination at the transitory whim of individual taste and fashion, so many excrescences have been added which are entirely wrong in style, so many plain, sensible features, walls, roofs, window frames, ripped out. It is not a question of my liking or not liking open-plan living or picture-windows. When you buy an old house, you buy a small part of the past, a piece of history, and yet you do not become the owner of that, and never can, you have only taken it on trust for your lifetime or, more likely nowadays, until you move on and pass it to someone else, in a cash transaction. You have every legal right, preservation orders withstanding, to alter and take down and put up, to imprint your own personality, to wrench a house into a new shape to fit your own living requirements. But no moral right at all.

Sensitive, cautious work, done to maintain and, indeed, to modernise, is one thing, but the rest ought only to be undertaken after a period of waiting and considering, and then advisedly, in the right spirit. That is the traditional attitude which has, at least some of the time, prevailed among the British landowning aristocracy, who have regarded possession of so many great architectural monuments as a family responsibility, a trust. But, as well as the castles and the great houses, our national heritage lies in all those modest, small-scale public and domestic buildings that still remain in the villages of Great Britain. The face of the country has been altered too much already. But a new spirit of conservation is abroad, a belated realisation that what is left ought to be more carefully preserved and tactfully treated. History is not buildings, it is people, but it is through buildings and, most especially, in their houses, that generations of those people have expressed themselves and left evidence of their way of life, its pattern and values. The least we owe to our ancestors is to make our own visual statements as gracefully and harmoniously and practically, as in keeping with the landscape around us, as possible, and to treat what we have inherited from the past with a proper respect. Which is not to say that clocks should be put back, or modern improvements outlawed from all but modern buildings, that people should again suffer darkness and damp and draughts, isolation and cramped discomfort, return to the hand plough and the village pump, and put up with the inefficient and ugly simply because it is old.

We painted most of the interior of Moon Cottage white, to reflect even more light; it makes all the humps and bumps of the old plasterwork, the funny slopes and levels, throw interesting shadows. We stripped old varnish from the beams in the kitchen and sitting room, and from the thick wooden arch over the fireplace where the range once would have stood, and then they were all sanded down very carefully until we arrived at a colour like acacia honey. We left the big, uneven stone flags in the entrance hall, although they strike cold in winter, but got rid of those candle-drip wall-lights. We can, alas, do nothing about the hideous mock-stone garage at the top of the steps except plant honeysuckle and the rose Albertine against it and feed them richly to make them grow well. I felt pleased, looking around me that day. But there is one drawback to Moon Cottage in winter, and that is the cold, the appalling cold borne in on all those winds from the Fen, and that first year we suffered from it and worried about what it cost us to try to alleviate the misery, for open fires do not give off enough heat, and we were dependent, for hot water and warmth, upon oil. Oil is smelly and costly and bulky to store, and its availability is often uncertain.

And then I bought our trusty little wood-burning stove and, a few weeks later, discovered Mr Ash. Winter life in Moon Cottage was transformed.

If you want anything in Barley you go to see Nance and George. Nance and George between them can find anyone who does anything, or sells it or sometimes has a bit of this in exchange for a bit of that. They know everyone in the village and for miles around, they relay advice, information and news. Nance runs her family and the village shop and delivers meals-on-wheels and is the Secretary of the W.I., George is caretaker of the village hall, a spare-time carpenter and handyman, a keeper of ferrets, shooter of pigeons and crows. He knows where and when you can get bales of straw, second-hand chicken wire, sloes, day-old bantams and green walnuts, retriever puppies, marrow plants and well-rotted manure. He has helped us out of trouble with our septic-tank overflow and a jackdaw-blocked chimney, got us a cheap garden shed and wrung the necks of sick hens. George is very tall and very thin, Nance is tiny, brittle-looking as a sparrow. I have never seen either of them sitting down. They have a stream running through the bottom of their garden, and, in spite of the ferrets, they rear orphaned leverets and ducklings and injured tawny owls. There is generally a makeshift cage or wire-run about the place, and a notice on garage or shed door saying 'Do not open'. I like to go and see them, they are good people to be with. And so, naturally, when I needed to locate a regular supply of wood for the stove, I went to ask them.

'Wood warms you twice, I say,' said George, resting for a second from cutting up his own logs. 'Once when you saw it up and then again when you burn it up.'

It was a sparkling day, the sky was blue as a blackbird's egg and crackling with frost, all the grasses and reeds of the hedges and ditches were iced and laced about with white, and all along the fence, at George's back, the spiders' webs were like spun sugar. Our breath smoked and his fingers were red as plums. 'Man you want,' he said, 'is Amos Ash.' He pointed. 'Green bungalow, beyond High Halt.'

Right. I reached the gate. 'Only trouble is,' he threw over his shoulder, 'he'll not answer his door.'

High Halt lies at the top of the ridge that runs above Barley for seven miles and overlooks all the villages of the Fen, and beyond. You go past the pond and then up a steep slope between overhanging trees, along a track which is a good place for blackberries in autumn and elderflowers in June, and where the ground is deeply scored with the marks of horseshoes, for the ridge is a glorious place to ride over. Over a stile, and then, abruptly, you are out on top.

This was a perfect day for being up there, the sky clear and cloudless, so that I could see for miles on all sides. The wind made a high, keening sound. On either side of the ridge itself are open fields, unfenced and at this time of year either ploughed or left to grass. Flocks of plovers were feeding and I saw several pheasants scurry for cover. I walked past the farm. No sign of a bungalow. So I went back and asked a man mending a post. He nodded down the slope to a copse lying low behind the farm paddock. I was a few yards on when he whistled. 'Doesn't answer his door.'

I went along a scruffy path towards an ugly, green-roofed, pebble-dashed bungalow set in a clearing just in front of the copse, the sort of house that was built just before planning permission, building regulations and green belt conservation got stricter. In front and on two sides was a sort of yard. Old water butts and oil drums and piles of assorted stakes, poles and logs, were littered about. Thin cats streaked away in all directions, and flattened themselves under doors. The net curtains at the windows were yellow, the paintwork flaking. A dog began to howl, and hurl itself at some closed doors.

I knocked once, hurriedly, and when no one came, scribbled my name and address on an old envelope with 'Please contact about logs', and pushed it through the letter flap. A snarl on the other side, a body hit the door, and my note disappeared. I ran, before any of the Starkadder family could emerge, determined that I would look elsewhere for my wood supplies.

The stove is not very large, and not very beautiful, but after it has been on for a day and a night, and the iron has heated through, it gives off a wonderful warmth that fills the entire ground floor of the cottage and rises up the staircase to the landing and bathroom immediately above. As we dislike hot bedrooms, this means that we need no longer use the central heating at all. But we *do* need a large and regular wood supply, and although I found I could buy a sackful here and there, no one else for miles around sold quantities of logs and would deliver them regularly. For two weeks we used anthracite on the stove and I hated it, hated the smell, the smuts, the nasty black piles of the stuff filling the store house. Then, one afternoon, the doorbell rang.

'Ash,' he said.

He wore a cap with the peak at the back of his head, and a raincoat with a piece of knotted string for a belt. String tied up his trousers at the knees. He was small and his face was the colour and texture of dried-out bark. At the top of the steps was a wooden hand-cart with long handles, and I began to explain that we had a greedy stove and would need lorry-loads of logs. He gave me a pitying look.

'Wants to sample, doesn't you?'

'Well, yes. . . .'

'Let's have a look at 'en.'

He came inside, opened the top of the stove, blew inside it, banged down the lid. Went outside again, glanced up at the chimney. Nodded.

'You don't want nothing green.'

I didn't?

'Tar,' he said, pityingly again, and went to fetch a sack of logs.

'Ash,' he said, 'Seven and six', and then another, 'Birch,' he said, 'nine bob', and then a third, 'Apple,' he said, 'and them's for your hearth, you don't waste apple on that stove. Nine bob.'

It is astonishing how completely I have forgotten the L.s.d. system. Seven and sixpence? Nine bob? I don't know how Mr Ash goes on with his shopping for he will have nothing whatsoever to do with the decimal system, and I have a struggle when he leaves the bit of old cigarette packet in the letter box that reads, 'Wood £11. 17/6d'.

He comes on alternate Mondays in winter, starting and stopping the deliveries when he himself decides, in accordance with the weather. He drops the logs into the shed, pushes his account through the door, closes the gate. He rarely speaks and his cap is always backwards. I thought he had a low opinion of us and our over-fed, hearth-rug cats. But at Christmas there was a gift, a great cherry log, with a sprig of holly stuck into the bark, left outside the back door. It burned evenly and steadily, as sweetly as the most fragrant pipe tobacco, scenting the whole house, and I was secretly pleased to discover from George and Nance that Mr Ash only hands out those to a few, favoured customers.

Whereas handling coal and its derivatives is unpleasant, I find handling wood very satisfying indeed, even on raw, wet mornings when I trudge down to the shed and pile the logs for the day into the wheelbarrow, with aching fingers. They feel right to the touch and weigh a good, solid weight, and I have been learning to tell one kind from another, and how seasoned it is. I can understand the pleasures of being a woodman, like Mr Ash, though I doubt if there are many like him around. But what I should like above all is to own some woodland myself, an acre or two of that precious, broad-leaved woodland which is vanishing at such an alarming rate. If I had enough money and a small wood were up for sale I should buy it, to ensure its survival, to preserve and care for the existing trees and plant new ones, to give habitat to its wildlife and flora, and help preserve those, too, for the future, and to walk in myself and look out upon through the seasons, for woods are a pleasure, and interesting and beautiful, all through the year, their personality changes subtly from month to month. Once the wood stove is lit, in October, we do not let it out again until April. The open fire is different, we have that not so much when we need it as when we can spend an evening sitting beside it, enjoying the smell and the sight of its burning, staring into it, poking and probing and rearranging it, for a wood fire is an activity, not an object to be admired passively. And to get the fire going is either the work of a few moments, if the wind is in the right, north-easterly direction, or of an hour of cursing and coaxing, if it blows south-west. Apart from the draught, the secret of success with it is in the laying, and in having the right sort of kindling to begin with; and that depends on going down the lane, to search about in the deep ditches. It is a thickly tree-lined, heavily overgrown lane that runs from Moon Cottage away from the village, down towards Sheep Hill and the Fen; old, fallen branches are propped up between the living ones and the ditches are full of dead wood. It takes me twenty minutes or so of rooting about and pulling and breaking each morning, to gather the kindling, and a very pleasant time it is. The dog Tinker loves it better than I do, for he digs and burrows and delves, emerging backwards from all manner of holes, with a filthy muzzle and an eager expression.

I always try to bring just a bit more wood than I need, to store in the shed for the wet days, or the days when I am going away; country people in the past never overlooked a good bit of kindling lying in their way, and rarely let a day go by, even in high summer, without giving a thought to their fuel store.

Well, we are not so dependent now, and wouldn't like to be so. But when I have found a particularly good, brittle old branch and broken it up into kindling sticks, or contemplated the old shed, stacked neatly with logs after Mr Ash has been, I still feel a sense of security, that we shall be warm no matter what, I look around the countryside defiantly, then, challenging the wind and weather to do their worst.

I am happy in most weathers, the variety, from day to day, of our climate, suits me, I should not be happy in any country where you could predict for months ahead that it would be dry and hot, or cool and wet, or cold and snowbound. I like the winter as well as any other time, and though it can be a test of endurance in some ways, it does bring a good many compensating pleasures.

Food

I HAVE ALWAYS seen the kitchen as the real heart of the house, and there is something delightfully warm, in all senses, about kitchen-living in winter. Until we moved to Barley, I had small kitchens, narrow, functional, overcrowded kitchens for working not for living in, packed out with cupboards and sinks and washing machines, and without any room for chairs and tables and a bookshelf. One of my basic requirements in any country house was to have as large a kitchen as possible. When I walked into the one at Moon Cottage, I knew that, short of a farmhouse-sized kitchen, I would not find anything better. It is big and square, with a walk-in larder and plenty of other cupboards, tucked into the walls, and we have filled it with furniture made of well-worn, plain wood, a dresser, a sideboard, a long table and chairs, an elm rocker, a great set of shelves. They do not exactly match one another, they have simply settled down happily and harmoniously, side by side. I have a particular loathing of 'fitted kitchens', especially in old houses, and country houses, they are so boring, lacking in personality, out of keeping.

The only thing I lack is a range, a great, comforting Aga or Rayburn on which to simmer soup and tea-kettles all day long, by which the animals could have their baskets and I could read in the rocking chair, a range which would be as welcome as the little wood-stove to the first person downstairs on a January morning. I have a long-term plan for my range. Otherwise, I am entirely content with and in Moon Cottage kitchen. Sometimes, when the house is empty, I bring my work down on to the long wooden table and write there. We begin the day there, in our morning scramble, and re-assemble again in the early evening, and in between times people call in and have cups of tea and Jessica does her painting and pastry-rolling, the cats tumble about on the floor and the table gets covered with mugs and vegetables and books and mixing bowls, with flour and crayons and bread-boards. I sit by myself ironing, and peeling, chopping and simmering, while listening to the wireless, or else the room is quite quiet except for the moan of the wind at the door and the tick of the clock on the wall.

In winter, I often spend all day in the kitchen, it is in winter that I love it best, and it is then that I most enjoy my own particular sort of cooking best, too, for one of the richest pleasures of domestic life is, and has always been, filling the house with the smells of food, of baking bread and cakes, bubbling casseroles and simmering soups, of vegetables fresh from the garden and quickly steamed, of the roasting of meat, of new-ground coffee and pounded spices and chopped herbs, of hot marmalade and jam and jelly.

The cooking I like to do is not what you might call 'best' cooking, not dinner-party or restaurant-style food. I leave all that to Stanley, who taught himself to cook superbly by reading the masters of French cuisine and taking all the trouble they expect you to take.

What I like is chopping up a great variety of vegetables for soup, and kneading bread and boiling jam, I like using beans and pulses, rice and lentils and pasta, rolling out wholemeal pastry, bottling and toffee-making and finding new ways of using up the vegetables as they come in their gluts. I like store-cupboard (not freezer) cooking, cooking in great quantity, cooking for feasts and festivals.

But, particularly now, I like cooking what I have grown in the garden. If we had more land, I should like to be self-sufficient not only in vegetables but in fruit, and also to provide poultry not just for eggs, as we do now, but for the table, and to keep a pair of goats for milk and cheese. Meanwhile, I try to grow a lot of what we especially enjoy eating, and which is not always easy to buy – and certainly not garden-fresh.

High on that list in winter comes celeriac, that knobbly, turnip-shaped, unappetising-looking root, which deserves to be better known. Cookery books, even those specialising in vegetable dishes, often do not mention it at all, or can give only a couple of recipes for it; mainly, they treat it just as a substitute for celery itself. But, although it has more or less the same, wholly distinctive, nutty flavour, celeriac is a fine vegetable in its own right. You can grate it raw, dress it in lemon juice, and serve it in winter salads, and celeriac soup is easily made, and delicious served with wholemeal bread. But the ways we most frequently have it are either as a purée (boiled, together with some potatoes, and afterwards mashed or sieved together, with some butter, a little cream or top of the milk, salt and pepper), or buttered. (Cut a celeriac into cubes of 1½" or so, plunge into boiling water for 12–15 minutes, or until tender but still firm. Drain and dry well on kitchen paper. Melt some butter in a heavy pan, and turn the celeriac in this over a low heat until well-covered. Add chopped parsley, a little lemon juice, salt and freshly ground black pepper.) Both these recipes for celeriac are good with any plain roast or grilled meat – especially game. (Stanley says venison too, but I have never been able to bring myself to eat this.)

Incidentally, celeriac is richer in iron than any other vegetable, including spinach, and so especially valuable for children and expectant mothers. Jessica chews it raw.

Red cabbage is another favourite winter standby, and so beautiful to look at, its colour dark as burgundy, and its interior, like those of the pomegranate or the Chinese gooseberry, one of nature's best bits of evidence for the existence of a Creator.

I make a huge pot of a red cabbage dish which is an amalgam of various recipes, and re-heat it over several days, until it gets dark and sticky and thick as jam. I am the only member of the family who likes it, which is nice for me, but I go on making it in vast quantities partly because I enjoy the soothing preparation of slicing all the cabbage and love filling the kitchen with a most marvellous smell. Jessica also likes it because it stains my fingers purple and that makes her laugh.

Red Cabbage

Quarter, core and finely shred a red cabbage. Peel, core and chop one or two apples (eaters or cookers), chop one onion, and one clove of garlic (optional).

Melt 1 oz butter in a big, heavy casserole. Add cabbage and cook gently with the lid on for about 5 minutes.

Then add apples, onion, garlic, some herbs such as a bayleaf, chopped parsley and thyme, two tablespoons of brown sugar, a small teacup of wine or cider, or half that quantity of wine vinegar, lots of salt and black pepper, and a little grated nutmeg.

Cook in a low oven for 3–4 hours, but check it after each hour and add a little water (or wine and water or cider,) if it is drying up.

Even better re-heated.

This goes beautifully with any plain meat, especially cold, and brightens up the cold poultry after Christmas. Also good with sausages. I like it just by itself.

I wish there were some way I could decorate the winter kitchen with more vegetables but we do have the onions hanging from a hook on the oak beam above the kitchen fireplace. I do not grow onions, we buy them, in great heavy strings, not, alas, from a Breton with beret and bicycle, but from a greengrocer in Stratford-upon-Avon, and they please me greatly, with their warm, reddish brown skins and plaited straw.

Because the sight of so many foods is similarly attractive, I keep rows of glass jars full of dried beans and lentils and rice ranged on open wooden shelves; black-eyed and dark red kidney beans, orange and earthy brown lentils, lettuce-green flageolets and chick peas the colour of cornmeal; the jars have cork stoppers and are practical as well as pretty, because we have never altogether cured the damp in Moon Cottage, and the larder is not a good place for storing any dried goods in packets.

Many people have prejudices against beans and grain, not

because they dislike the flavour – their experience of them may well be limited – but because of the cranky bean image, which seems to go with vegetarianism, sandals and strange religious cults. I do understand. But there are so many delicious and even sophisticated ways of serving them, and their variety, cheapness and nutritional value cannot easily be dismissed.

I have always made a lot of soup in winter, we have it virtually every day, with meat-based stocks, from the weekend carcase, or tenpence worth of butcher's bones. (It is not true that you can no longer get these, in town or city; our nearest Co-op butcher has them ready-packed up, beef, pork or bacon, and any butcher will gladly chop up a handful, and if you are buying something else, may well give them to you free.) But, whatever the base, I generally add a handful of lentils, or split peas, or haricot beans, along with whatever vegetables are to hand, and there are a lot of thick, savoury soups to be made quickly and simply, with beans or lentils or both, as the main ingredient. Our weekend lunches in winter usually consist of this, with a heap of grated cheese to sprinkle on top, and chunks of brown bread.

If, on Saturday or Sunday, we go for a walk, we love to come home to tea, a proper tea, with banana or walnut and apple bread, sliced, with butter on, and perhaps griddle cakes or scones and jam and shortbread. I rarely make puddings, except when we have visitors, so we do not feel too greedy.

Just after the war, my mother bought a Yorkshire Women's Institute Cookery Book, a collection of recipes from country ladies all over that home county of mine (as well as household hints on how to get rid of various stains, or cure ham or make furniture polish or treat burns and scalds). One of the nicest recipes was for nut and apple tea-bread; my mother often made it and now I do, though I use soft margarine, which was not available in her day, and I have passed the recipe round the village, too, after being complimented on the loaf at a W. I. meeting. It is best made a day before eating, or it crumbles too easily when cut, and you don't have to put butter on it, because it is already rich and very filling.

Walnut and apple tea-bread

2 oz walnuts, chopped
1 large cooking apple
4 oz soft margarine or butter
4 oz raisins
4 oz brown sugar
2 eggs
1 tablespoon honey
6 oz S. R. flour
2 oz wholemeal flour
Pinch mixed spice if liked (I don't)
Pinch salt
Use two lb loaf tins. Line with greased greaseproof paper. Peel, core and chop the apple. Then place everything in a mixing bowl and beat for 2 minutes, by hand or with an electric beater. Pour into the tins. Bake for 1 hour at Electricity 350 (180 C) or Gas 4. Reduce heat to Electricity 325 (160 C) Gas 3, for 20 minutes more. Test with a skewer and if still gooey in the middle, cook on, if necessary covering the top with foil, for another 10 minutes. Turn out on to a wire rack to cool.

All the winter food I prepare and eat I find satisfying to the eye and the nostrils, as well as the palate and stomach, but Christmas food crowns it all with glory, it is at Christmas that I always wish we had a great barn of a house and could fill it with twenty friends, for the food cries out to be made in quantity, and to be displayed on a Victorian cornucopia of groaning tables.

Because more of the joy is, for me, in the preparation than in the actual eating, I always make far too much for us to eat. Never mind, for it is a pleasure to give it away, to tie red ribbon around jars of home-made mincemeat and present an extra cake or pudding or a dish of mince-pies to an elderly neighbour or to the Christmas bazaar.

I try new recipes each year, though my mother baked all her

cakes without using recipes at all; perhaps it was just as well, because she had to save up the precious rationed ingredients for months beforehand, and some were simply unobtainable, so inventiveness and ingenuity ruled.

Last Christmas Eve was crisp and cold and bright and we were going carol singing in the evening, so that I wanted to have mince-pies and sausage rolls ready to contribute to what we would all scoff afterwards. The kitchen was smelling wonderfully aromatic, of warm pastry and brandy and mincemeat, and it was very hot, too. Jessica seemed oddly subdued and a little flushed, as she rolled her own piece of shortcrust pastry to within an inch of its life, but then, so was I flushed, and I didn't take much notice. The first batch of pies was cooling on the wire rack when the window-cleaners arrived – not a pair of them, as usual, but four, and wanted some milk for their tea, and gazed at the mince-pies like hungry schoolboys until I offered them and they took two each, so I had to start on more pastry. Then a friend from the other side of the village brought a Christmas fruit loaf dusted with icing sugar and tied in yellow ribbon and a cloth, and told us her goat had got out and if we saw it . . . and then another neighbour with two small sons and a party invitation arrived and the kettle went on and more pies disappeared and the kitchen was packed with happy people and Jessica was looking even more flushed, and I was thinking of bringing out the plum brandy and turning the whole thing into a party when a window-cleaner shouted through an opened window that there was a man outside with a crateful of hens. And so there was, our hens had arrived in time for Christmas, and everyone came out to look and admire their creamy whiteness and see them installed in the hen house, and suddenly the hall was full of sacks of layers' mash and corn and a bale of straw and over the wireless came the first of the Nine Lessons and Carols from King's College, Cambridge.

By the time everyone had left, nearly two dozen of the mince-pies and a lot of sausage rolls had been consumed and there were none for us or the carol singers. I heaved another bag of flour out of the larder and Jessica went off to watch 'Play School' and fell asleep over it, still oddly flushed. By the time I set off for the church in my scarf and boots, I never wanted to see another spoonful of mincemeat, and there was a goat in the garden.

The next morning, we woke early, to the sound of the bells pealing Christmas through the village. It was another golden day, of frosty cold and brilliant sunshine. A hen had laid one egg for Christmas and Jessica was entirely covered in little pink spots.

Because of the measles, the friends who were to have come for Christmas did not, and Stanley and I ate our celebration dinner alone together, in the evening. We had roast pheasant with celeriac purée and watercress salad, home-made basil and apple jelly and a fresh pineapple, and finally, on New Year's Day, the traditional Christmas dinner with a lot of friends and their children. The turkey was a free-range, whole-food bird from a farm in the next village which produces all sorts of poultry for the table. The difference between that and the battery (let alone that abomination, the frozen) bird was for all to taste in every succulent mouthful. Besides, if I am going to eat meat, I like to know the animal has had a decent, and natural, life before being killed. It is rarely indeed that I am convinced it has.

The following week, on a blustery, wet day of racing clouds, I declared the kitchen out of bounds to all and spent a peaceful time making the marmalade. We have three kinds, a thick, dark Oxford, a few jars of a special liqueur whisky marmalade, and plain seville orange with the peel cut very thinly. The fruity smells, and the sight of the jars lined up, tawny-gold and translucent on the table, gave a glow to January. I looked out of the window at the bending trees and low cloud and thought how exactly right the job was for the time, warming and colourful, absorbing and satisfying in the drear, dark season – the epitome of 'winter cooking'.

Festivals

THE COUNTRY year is marked by the changes in the weather and the look of the landscape, the Church's year by the cycle of the Church calendar, and the village year has its own pattern, too, following both, and including all the social festivals and community activities, and so the wheel turns, for everything there is a season. I would not want to have the leaves fall in June, or the fruits ripen in March, to eat plum pudding on a blazing hot day or see the peas fat in their pods in the kitchen garden in snow. Naturally not, who would? The same people who want chrysanthemums all the year round and frozen raspberries on bonfire night, that's who, and they have been gaining ground, trying to regularise and standardise, and alter the natural, productive cycle of the year to suit themselves, to force and freeze. But there is, and always has been, a quiet resistance movement, and in all the villages of Britain you find the pattern of the year's feasts and festivals and seasonal celebrations meticulously followed, and the fruits of the earth enjoyed also in their turn.

Every day, from around the middle of October, you may see people going up the lanes of the village pushing wheelbarrows, old prams or bicycles with baskets, laden with all manner of burnable refuse. Guy Fawkes night comes at a useful time for gardeners, everyone is clearing up. The pushers and pullers heave up the steep hill that runs out of the village to the east, Norman Lane, at the top of which is the football field on which the Youth Club and the Cubs and Scouts will construct that wondrous edifice, the Barley Bonfire.

When it is finally piled up and propped around with planks, like a vast wigwam, a roster of security guards will be drawn up to protect it from the raiding parties sent out by rival villagers, and there is a huge tarpaulin on hand, in case of really prolonged rain.

Because the field is at the top of the hill, and there are wide views all the way round, the Barley Bonfire is also lit to celebrate Royal and National events. But the Guy Fawkes one comes at the best time of all, it has a pagan magic that draws all who can make the climb to the top, to stand in a wide circle around the fire as it roars up and the sparks and smoke fly free. Someone brings hot soup in an urn and dishes it out from the back of an estate wagon, others have baskets of bread rolls and sausages kept hot in foil, and there are toffee apples for the children.

Away from the light of the fire, at the edges of the field, is darkness, and you creep away from it, nearer to the warmth and the people, understanding why primitive man huddled around the sticks he had learned how to burn. As we walk back home through the village, the smell of the bonfire merges with the smoke from everyone's chimney, and when we get indoors and hang up our coats and scarves, the smokiness clings to them, too, and the next morning there is the smell of old ash and charred earth on the wind. There is a smell to every season, and smoke outdoors is the smell of November.

The Church, of course, doesn't mark Guy Fawkes night, but a few days before come those twin days of darkness and light, gloom and gladness, All Saints' and All Souls' Day, and early December brings Advent, and a special service in Barley Church on Advent Sunday, to mark the real beginning of Christmas, when the village children carry in candles, to provide the only light for the singing of the advent hymn.

December the sixth is the feast of St. Nicholas and, as Barley Church is dedicated to him, there is a St. Nicholas feast and in places of honour at the table that runs cross-wise to the other two are the choir, for St. Nicholas is the patron saint of choirboys – though our church, like many another now, has as many girls as boys, as many ladies as men, in the parish choir. The feast takes place in the church itself. So does the Parish harvest supper. We set out trestle tables in an oblong shape, at the spacious back of the church, by the font and beneath the bell rope, which is tied up out of reach for the occasion. Choir parents, members of the Parochial Church Council and senior citizens of Barley are guests of honour, too, and everyone is served by the Women's Institute members and other parish ladies, who have prepared the food and drink in their own kitchens during the afternoon and brought it up in baskets. There are jugs of cider, and orange squash, there are cold meat pies and hot potatoes in their jackets, trifles and ginger cakes and bowls of nuts and sweets. The tables are laid with white cloths and decorated with holly from the churchyard and with wonderful chrysanthemums, great pom-poms of white and butter-yellow and rust red, grown by Mr Elder, who has won cups and trophies with them up and down the country for years. There is a grace, and a thanksgiving hymn sung by the choir, at their places, and a lot of laughter. It is an unusual occasion, personal to us, simple, joyful, traditional, the first of all the parties.

Barley is a very party-minded village, there is always much to-ing and fro-ing between houses, with people wearing their finery under overcoats, cars full of excited children emptying on to doorsteps. Nearly everyone has a lighted Christmas tree in the window and a holly wreath tied with red ribbons on the front door, and there are often little parcels on doorsteps, pots of preserves tied with a bow on top or bottles of home-made wine and cider and sloe gin.

But the best of the Christmas celebration is the carol singing on Christmas Eve. Though it doesn't seem quite so jolly on the three previous Wednesday evenings, when those who cannot cook up any excuse gather in the church for a practice. It is icy cold, dark and empty, and we keep on our coats and our hands ache holding the song sheets and our voices sound piping and odd, lost among the stone recesses of the old building. There are funny, scrabbling noises in corners, and that dank, musty smell. We huddle under the pulpit. No one is very enthusiastic. Well, perhaps better leave it there, says the choirmaster, who is really a dentist, 'But do keep practising at home. . . .' But, within seconds, he is talking to himself, everyone has scattered off home to lamps and fires and hot toddies.

Atmosphere, that's all the practices lack really, the atmosphere of Christmas Eve, excitement, the sense of occasion which pulls everyone together and lifts up our hearts and our voices. I always say we should abandon them altogether. It isn't as if the carols are unfamiliar to anyone, and they not only depress the singers, they cause half of us to catch cold and miss the event itself.

Christmas Eve comes. This year it came cold; frost lay hard as iron, the gutters and taps hung with icicles like sugar sticks and all the rooftops and stone walls, the garden fences and the gravestones, gleamed phosphorescent, like silver snails' trails, where it had rained a little that morning and then suddenly frozen. Our breaths plumed out on the air, our footsteps rang, the stars prickled. There was that curious crackling feel to the atmosphere as it touched face and fingers. Barley lay, empty and beautiful under the frost-rimmed moon. Behind closed doors and curtained windows, in firelight and lamplight, people waited.

The singers arrived, and there was much blowing on hands and stamping and sucking of those red winter cough drops that smell of paraffin and cloves, and then, piling out of cars and off bicycles, the players, mostly older children who belong to a nearby silver band; a trombone and two trumpets, a clarinet, several recorders, a saxophone; the leader played the flute and had a music stand borne ahead of her and set down at each stopping place by two eager pupils. More puffing and blowing and tuning up, a lot of throat clearing. The vicar, wreathed in mufflers, said a prayer, gave a blessing, went home, coughing, and we were off, to the corner of the Old Manor House, and by the almshouses, down as far as old Miss Reevers, whose dog barked, though she herself gave no sign that she had heard us; back up the lanes, marching hard, laughing and chatting, joined on the way by latecomers, and various children. We sang 'O Come all ye Faithful' at the Fox and Feathers, under their ten-foot-high, lighted Christmas tree, and 'See Amid the Winter Snow' beside the iced-over pond. We wished a Merry Christmas and a Happy New Year to ninety-three-year-old Mr Stump, who adjusted his hearing aid up and down, and got his wife, who is ninety-seven, to stand on a chair and open the window wide, and greeted a new baby at Fen Farm with 'Away in a Manger'. Our fingers were stiff with cold and our voices raw as cheese-graters. The church clock struck ten. Some of the children were taken home. It was colder still, too cold for snow. We were glad to get to the Manor House again, and pile into the hall in the old way, for mince-pies and sausage rolls and punch and the blaze of the fire on our frozen faces. The lights went out, except for those of the tree. 'Silent Night', which brings tears to the eyes. A second or two of absolute silence, before the bursting of a log up like a firework and down again in a great golden shower of sparks. Laughter and lights again and a Happy Christmas, a Happy Christmas, and a Happy Christmas floating faint on the freezing air down all the lanes and home.

Wildlife

WATCHING BIRDS was not something we began to do when we moved into the country. We had an extraordinary variety of bird life in our town gardens, particularly in winter; in our Stratford-upon-Avon lilac tree, a pair of blackcaps used to over-winter, and during the harsh weather of 1979, we surprised a flock of fieldfares trying to scratch under the rose-beds in the middle of North Oxford; when I had a tree outside my study window in Leamington Spa, a tree-creeper crept past me each morning, delving for insects. Town birds are, on the whole, tamer and bolder than country birds, and because the garden of Moon Cottage is open to the country on three sides, and has a wilderness behind the derelict cottage next door, we see far more birds from a distance, going about their lives unaffected by humans and their habitations, than we used to. But we still feed them in the cold weather as religiously as ever.

The fact that we have two cats ought, perhaps, to deter us. But we are not trying to tame birds, or encourage them to get very close to the house, by using special, windowsill feeders, merely providing the supplies against winter famine, and enjoying watching them from afar. The senior cat, Hastings the tabby, could probably still catch a bird if she really tried, and if it was stationary for long enough, but she is very fat and old and half-blind, and presents little serious threat. Polly is young, lithe, lean and black, and would catch anything. We make sure we do not put any food on the ground, around the house-area, only feed on a bird-table hanging high in the apple tree, or on the top of the old willow-stump. Of course she could catch them there, but the height and the distance give them a warning and a chance to escape. We keep her extra-well fed, do not put anything at all down when the fledglings are about; the other factor is the presence of field mice and voles in the wild garden next door, in the copse beyond it, and in all the fields below the house, which provide ample sport.

Last winter, I kept a careful record, for a week, of the bird-life in and around Moon Cottage. There were no really rare sightings, though one or two unusual events, and it proved to be fairly representative. Down on the Fen, and especially in the wilder bits, far more unusual birds are sighted, especially on migration-and as winter visitors. In wet winters or during a heavy thaw, the whole area can be flooded for weeks on end. Curlews come, and various kinds of duck, including shelduck and pintail, shoveller and wigeon. There have even been occasional reports of smew and white-fronted geese. We have seen none of them because we are just too far away to get a clear, detailed view, with the binoculars, and the Fen is inaccessible on foot, or horseback, or in a vehicle, when it is flooded; but this does mean that the birds can rest there absolutely undisturbed, though bang in the centre of a well-farmed, well-populated area of countryside.

Sunday

Made a bird pudding. I melt half a pound of lard, with some bacon rind and scraps, in a pan. Mix in wild bird nuts and seed, toast, bread and cereal crumbs, a few miscellaneous table scraps, finely chopped, until the whole is of a porridgey consistency. This is spooned into two half-coconut shells, packed down hard and left to cool and congeal thoroughly. Garden wire is then threaded through a hole in the shell and the whole thing suspended from the top of the fencing opposite the kitchen window, and from a branch of the apple tree. It will take about five days, less if the weather is severe, for the shells to be scraped absolutely shining clean.

Monday

The bird pudding shells are constantly frequented, with a sort of running queue forming on the fence, and rooftops, of waiting birds.

This morning there have been blue, great and coal tits, and on the apple tree shell, farther from the comings and goings of the house, a marsh or willow tit (I find them indistinguishable). The resident garden robin waits until the tits have stopped their bobbing and fussing for a few moments, and then hops down and feeds swiftly and purposefully, before the next invasion.

Sparrows, wrens, greenfinches and chaffinches are all expert peckers at the shells, each taking their preferred tit-bit, but the starlings strut about on the ground, apparently oblivious of the treats overhead.

Tuesday

The Buttercup and Dovehouse fields beyond the cottage are thick with fieldfares and redwings flocking and feeding together, as usual in our sort of farmland, during the winter. If the weather gets very harsh, the fieldfares may well come into the garden next door to plunder the cotoneaster berries, but so far it has been merely grey and very wet, so they will have ample food.

Wednesday

A sudden drop in temperature drove away the low clouds, and on a bright, bitter, clear morning, I walked up to High Halt and along the ridge, and there I found the lapwings in their hundreds, in and out of the stubble. I have often thought that if lapwings were not so common and easily seen in great numbers, people would travel hundreds of miles to get a sight of them, because of their elegance, with long legs and graceful crest, and their startling and beautiful aerobatic displays in spring. So many rare birds are actually rather plain-looking.

There were also plenty of pheasants, running away at the sight and sound of me, to the shelter of the copses and hedges down the slope, for this is the dangerous time of year for them. There is some local shooting, though not on any grand organized scale. But I was at dinner next to a farmer from a dozen or so miles away, and when he said he had a large acreage of entirely arable land, I asked suspiciously if he had ripped out all his hedges and filled in the ditches, to make vast, E.E.C.-subsidized grain-prairies. He was a courteous and charming companion, and not at all put out by my aggressiveness, but said mildly that no, actually, his fields were amply large enough, he saw no point in being 'the richest man in the churchyard' and that he cared for wild-life. But, even more, he cared for shooting, and the hedgerows were essential cover for the birds. So perhaps shooting should be even more encouraged on farms and small estates, so that more hedgerows would be left intact.

Thursday

Last night was the coldest so far this winter, with a considerable frost. I woke at dawn in a sudden panic that I had forgotten to lock away the hens, and went out into the garden in dressing gown and wellingtons, to check. It was a marvellous morning, the branches of the trees, the fences and grass completely white, the sun coming up in a poppy-coloured ball, with a curious hoary beard around it, and the air as still as I have ever known it here, as though the very wind itself were frozen silent. The grass crisped softly under my feet.

The hens were locked up, and bumped down from their roosting perch as soon as they heard me, so I let them out and then went over to the shed to bring in a couple of logs to top up the stove. As I opened the broken door, there was a frantic rush of wings and small bodies, and at least ten wrens fled into the open. I climbed up on the pile of logs, and saw, high up in the groin of the roof, hidden deep in some ivy, a small hole, not much bigger than a 50 pence piece. There the wrens nested in spring, and there they had now gone to roost. I wondered how many of them might pack together if the weather stayed cold, for I have read reports of forty-odd birds huddled into astonishingly small spaces, for warmth – cold winters are death to many thousands of the tiny wrens, who have precious little reserves of flesh and feather to see them through. But the following week we discovered that several were actually roosting inside the house, getting through a very small hole in the window pane of the boiler and storeroom. They were there as dry and warm as could be, though not especially safe, for the door is often left open and the cats prowl.

Friday

Up against the ugly concrete wall of an old outbuilding of the derelict cottage next door is a vast cotoneaster, overgrown and rambling, and there are a good many others at this end of the village. I do not greatly care for them, but this winter the berries have been very thick, and a brighter sight, at least, than the porridge-coloured old concrete. This morning, I was standing at the sitting-room window, looking out at nothing in particular, when I caught a flash of brightly coloured plumage, and then another, in the next-door wilderness. Goldfinches? They seemed too large. But my short-sight is so bad now that I cannot trust myself without the binoculars. When I looked through them, I shrieked with excitement. Not goldfinches, but a flock of waxwings were stripping the cotoneaster systematically. Then I noticed a stray pair in our rowan tree, taking what few berries had been left by the other, marauding finches. The waxwings, with their marvellous red, black and yellow wings and little crested heads, stayed for perhaps fifteen minutes, and when they left, rising as one bird into the air, there was not a berry left on that great, sprawling bush. I heard later that they had raided almost every other cotoneaster in Barley, and some ornamental cherries too, before moving on.

Saturday

Of the birds regularly at our feeding station, blackbirds, chaffinches, thrushes, hedge and house sparrows, robin and tits and wrens, all are welcome, except starlings. I wage a one-woman war against them and their racket, their foul mess, their greed, their aggressiveness and generally cocky manner. A lot of people actually like their characters, and I know they are good scavengers in the fields – fine, let them go to the fields. But I have discovered a way to outwit them on the domestic front and that is to get up and put out the bird scraps and seed as early as possible. Starlings, as befits their general nature, are late risers, lying about in their nests well after all the other birds are on the wing. So by the time they descend in their bossy, rackety flocks the rest are well-fed and watered and there are only the crumbs and scrapings remaining for the latecomers.

Stanley points out mildly that they still *do* come. But at least they don't hog the place and do the other birds out of their meal.

This afternoon, I spent an hour or so clearing and tidying the general garden rubbish that we left at the wet end of the autumn, and as I went up and down and around, the robin came with me, in that companionable way of its kind, hopping from tree to wall to fence, and back again and singing his most rich and expansive song because of the winter sunshine. I talk to him, as I often do talk to the birds, but he is the only one who does not make me feel that such conversation is foolish, because he does seem to listen and to respond, he is aware of my friendly presence. I am reminded of the robin in that best of all children's books, *The Secret Garden*.

The stories of tame and intelligent robins abound. Our friend Kate, a few years ago, rescued an injured robin and kept him in her room for almost a year, until he was as knowing and biddable as any canary or parrot.

Just as I was preparing to go indoors, I heard a tremendous row around the far side of the house, and when I went to investigate, found our own robin seeing off another male who had dared to venture on to his territory, with a most fierce display, all puffed out chest feathers and high, angry pip-pip-pip. It took only a minute or two for him to make his point successfully, and then he sat half-way up the apple tree, consolidating his triumph.

*

I was working at my desk one Saturday morning in January when I heard the sound of the hunting horn very nearby; it had an extraordinary effect on me, stirring, exciting, so that I jumped up and ran outside, anxious to find out where they were. When I was a child, and a teenager, I rode a lot and hunted occasionally, though I was never very intrepid, and always followed along fairly far to the back, on a fat, sedate old pony, and went round all the gates and high hedges. But I enjoyed it, the whole colourful, lively event, the meet outside an Inn or Manor house, the way the very fresh horses were so giddy and restless, the trays of sandwiches and drinks, the admiring crowd, the spurt of fear and pleasure in your stomach as the huntsmen moved off, and then the chase over fields and getting cold and covered in mud and coming home aching and filthy, to bath and rest. I was not a bloodthirsty child – indeed, rather the contrary, but nevertheless I took the whole business of hunting calmly for granted, and never thought about the ethics of it. Man has always hunted, for food or sport or both, some primitive instinct is still aroused by the chase. We do have to control foxes and I doubt if there are any more humane methods, though actually, hunting is not particularly efficient. I scarcely remember a kill in my youth, and often we did not even find.

When I got outside into the garden of Moon Cottage, I heard the horn again, braying through the clear air, and then I saw them, streaming down the Buttercup field immediately below me, the whole marvellous array of them, men in pink, women in black, and the great strong horses and silly yelping hounds and, at the back, the little Thelwell girls with pigtails bouncing up and down, being steered clear of a particularly nasty ditch. They went over the fences and on up the Rise and for sixpence I could have gone with them, I wanted to have a horse again and fly and fly. . . .

When Stanley and Jessica came in I told them about it and, even then, my excitement hadn't died down. 'You should have seen them,' I said, 'it really is a magnificent sight.'

'I'm glad I didn't. All those men and slavering dogs giving one poor creature such terror, hell bent on cornering it and tearing it apart while it's still alive.'

And Jessica said, 'Oh, poor, poor Mr Fox,' and cried and cried, for she has the tenderest of hearts, even though that same fox is the villain of so many of her story books, even though she knows how many hens have been taken in the village this winter, and how he comes round every night, sniffing for ours.

Yes, yes, I thought, in my heart I know they are probably right, it *is* an unspeakable activity and unworthy of the dignity of man. And yet. . . . Finally, I sit on the fence.

There is a good story in the village about the time the hunt ended up in the garden of Mrs Miggs, aged ninety-four. Mrs Miggs lives in one of the oldest, low-lying cottages down Fen Lane, a narrow, thick-walled house with minute windows entirely obscured by indoor geraniums, gangly and overgrown. She has a sort of light-less inner parlour where she sits all day with her canary and her wireless which, because she is deaf, she has turned up very loud. On this particular day, she was happily installed, listening to the Jimmy Young Show, when the fox, followed close by the whole pack of hounds, broke through the hedge into her kitchen garden while the rest of the hunt milled about in the lane outside steaming and panting and horses pressed their great hind-quarters against the door and windows of the cottage, there was a tremendous racket, and the fox was finished off. It brought out everyone else in the lane but Mrs Miggs sat on, quite oblivious to all of it, doing her crochet and listening to the music.

The foxes in Barley have been getting more and more open-faced in their boldness this past winter. One Sunday morning, he went up the track into the stable-yard behind the Grange where Lavender keeps her hens running free and killed six right off, while everyone was singing 'Ye Holy Angels Bright' at morning service a few yards away. The following Sunday he went back at precisely the same time for the rest.

Lavender hunts twice weekly in winter and who could blame her for feeling bloodthirsty then, yet her heart being also soft at the core, when she saw an injured fox sitting in the middle of the orchard beyond her window her distress was great and she went all over the village to find a man with a gun who would come at once and put the poor creature down.

War by trap was waged after a very tame, very pet Muscovy duck was taken in Ellen's beautifully tended garden near the post box, and she caught seven foxes within a few weeks, but there were plenty more where they came from, in Foxley Spinney and Spoke Woods, and all the little copses around and about between Barley and the Fen, and the next week, the village school chickens were massacred and left lying all over the run headless, to the agony of the child in charge of locking them away at the time. I can forgive them for taking hens for food, but not for the fun of slaughter, and yet I wonder if it *is* only a desire to keep down the fox population which makes one respond, as I did, to the sound of the tally-ho?

When it has snowed, we see the fox tracks every morning, they run up our garden from the low wall, and around the hen run and then away up the stone steps and across the lane into the field opposite, he makes a regular, routine check, so that if we forget once to shut the door of the henhouse, he will pounce. On winter nights, too, we hear the eerie shrieks of the vixen down in the spinney below Sheep Hill, and the barks of the dog foxes fighting over her, they are sounds to chill the blood; to make you pull the curtains together more tightly and throw another log on the fire to make it blaze. Yet the fox would never harm a human, and when seen at close quarters he is no more alarming than a dog – I am always taken aback each time by how much smaller and slighter he is in reality than in my mind, where his villainous deeds and fierce sounds and all those stories about him have swollen him into monstrous size. And fox-cubs, like all young creatures, are quite enchanting. I shall never trust him nor encourage him to come near, but the country-side would be the poorer without him, for in the fox we have a villain and a scapegoat, something to remind us of the essential bloodiness of nature. In this quiet countryside, he is the nearest we get to all those ravening wolves and brute bears of the wild, and of legend.

The Garden

GARDENING WRITERS, I have come to the conclusion, live in some other world, an ideal land in which the weather always behaves as it should and is entirely predictable, month by month, season by season. So they say, December – by now you should have completed digging over the kitchen garden ready for those hard frosts of the new year to break down the clods of soil.

Excellent advice. It does not, however, allow for the spurt of weather we frequently have prior to Christmas, week after week of rain, which turns the ground into plasticine and makes all digging impossible. So January finds me beginning, rather than finishing, what is laughingly known as 'the autumn dig'. Then I have to do what you are told never to do, dig in a rush (bad for the back) in order to get it done on the few non-wet but also frost-free days available.

But it is a job I love, all the same, rhythmical and satisfying, with the robin for company and something to show at the end of it all, that line of mealy-brown, turned-over earth and all the mess of weeds nicely buried.

I keep resting, to look up and over the Fen, where the sky changes constantly, so that the colours and shadows are different every time, the fields of winter wheat and stubble and grassland are blue or grey, or else, suddenly, pale lemon and honey-coloured, as the sun strikes through. Sometimes, one, white-painted farmhouse at the top of Hope-on-the-Slope is picked out by its rays and the whiteness reflects and radiates, while all around, the hump of the Ridge and the wooded slopes, are slate-dark.

47

After digging come the other two jobs which smell so good, manuring and composting. The manure has been rotting for a year in John Plum's farmyard, the compost we make ourselves. There is always an anxious moment when the heaps are uncovered. If it hasn't heated up properly, or has been too wet or too dry, it will be a vile, lumpy slimy mess of worms and muck. But this year it was fine, crumbly brown-black and rich, I spread it over the soil, with the manure, and turned it lightly in, with much satisfaction.

When we arrived, the kitchen garden of Moon Cottage was a wilderness of couch grass and nettles and thistles, but when it was cleared and rotavated, we discovered hundreds of bulbs, mainly giant tulip, daffodil and narcissi, which had been established for years and were deeply rooted, huge as hands, fibrous and knotty. We had them all out, but the ground was sour and heavy and will need a good few years of intensive cultivation, plus all the manure and compost I can give it, before the vegetable yield will be anything to be proud of.

It is good soil in parts, but with bands of nasty, heavy, orangey clay, which makes impossible the growing of anything remotely delicate or temperamental.

If digging is the best winter job, clearing up is a chore I hate, akin to tidying the house; indeed, there are a good many garden jobs, like weeding, clipping, clearing and dead-heading, which come into the category of outdoor housework, but there are fewer of them in the kitchen garden than elsewhere, which is why I concentrate almost all my energies there, and leave the flowers, shrubs and grass to the rest of the family.

I don't grow a large variety of the more mundane winter vegetables, maincrop carrots, potatoes and onions, because there seems too little point, they take up such precious acres of space, and do not seem any poorer if we buy them from the market than if we pulled them fresh from our own garden, in the way that the spring and summer vegetables certainly do. Nor do I grow cabbages or sprouts (we loathe them) or cauliflowers (not on our soil).

I do always grow a lot of leeks, those entirely easy-going creatures, pleasing to behold as soldiers in the ground, resistant to all diseases and pests, tolerant of any soil, long-lasting, reliable. I like the fact that you don't have to pull leeks until you need them, they are quite happy sitting for ages in the ground, and that I can go and get just one or two, for soup or casserole, whereas I have to buy a whole pound from the market. They are my great winter standby, along with the celeriac, I could not be without them in garden or kitchen.

Nor, in March and April, would I be without purple- and white-sprouting broccoli (known in the greengrocery business, apparently, simply as 'purple sprouting'), picked when the shoots are young and tender as butter and steamed for only a few minutes until they turn that bright, artificial green which is a sign of the really fresh vegetable. These are scarcely any more trouble than leeks to grow. I use a couple of packets of seeds to bring on the plants, and put them in at the end of June or early July. They have to be planted deep and heeled in hard in our exposed garden, to protect them from wind-rock through autumn and winter, and I always have to go round them two or three times a week, picking off caterpillars.

If the worst comes to the worst, I spray, with one of the natural insecticides (i.e. those whose active ingredients are plant-based). These are excellent, they do work and sometimes, with particularly recalcitrant and damaging pests, it's the only answer. It would be splendid if one could follow the ecological line to the last in the kitchen garden and rely entirely on the natural order to keep one clear of pests. In practice, though, it is rarely enough, and so long as I am not trigger-happy with sprays, I don't allow myself to feel guilty about it.

There is never any real end to the year in the vegetable garden, things grow and produce right through the winter, and the end of one season overlaps with the beginning of the next. Only the worst of the weather causes a halt.

In early February come two pointers to spring and the start of the main growing season: seed potatoes and shallots arrive. I order mine, after much shopping around, from a reliable supplier of some more unusual varieties, because what I now aim to do is grow enough earlies to keep us going right through the summer, and to have a couple of rather rare kinds, with a main block of a proven, reliable early like Sharpe's Express or Maris Peer. I particularly like two lovely pink new potatoes, Vanessa and Pink Fir Apple, which, besides looking pretty, are wonderful for salads, and Epicure, which produces delicious, though often rather small, tubers. The search for unusual varieties is worthwhile, for the flavour of many of them, as well as of the commoner kinds, is incomparable.

So, in February, the windowsills of our bedrooms are covered in wooden crates full of seed potatoes being chitted, and at the end of the month, if it is not frosty or too wet, in go the shallots, another under-appreciated vegetable, hard to buy in the markets. I cannot understand why. They are easy to grow in most soils, and are trouble-free if you dust them against the dreaded onion fly when you first plant, they store well and are good in the kitchen because of their sweetness and mildness, and because they are small, when onions come so big that I am forever cutting them up and finding the soft, rotting halves at the bottom of the rack. And I like the nutty brown of the shallot skins, as they hang in their nets from a hook.

Last November, I planted some broad beans, having been told they wintered well, would be resistant to black fly and give us really early pods, probably in May. I protected the sowing from mice and pigeons by putting holly twigs along the rows (it pricks the mice's noses). What went wrong I do not know but I shan't try them again. The beans did get black fly, they were scarcely any earlier than the spring-sown variety and worst of all, doubtless because they endured all the awful weather like troopers, they were horribly tough.

Our other, regular winter vegetable is perpetual spinach (or spinach beet). One sowing in July, of three rows, provides us with regular pickings right round the year until April. I have pulled spinach in snow, in pouring rain, in howling gales, in the bitterest cold of January, and there has always been enough for the three of us, though of course growth is slower in the really extreme weather. It is no trouble at all, it never runs to seed like its neurotic summer cousin, all you have to do is keep it weed-free and keep picking. I have read that you should protect it with cloches against the frost, like parsley, but I have never done so, because it is so windy here that cloches, however apparently well-anchored, always end up at the bottom of the field or hanging from a telegraph wire in the lane, and the spinach, so far, has not let us down.

If I do precious little in the flower garden, that little is directed towards providing for what will give us the maximum reward for the minimum effort over the longest period, and into that category come bulbs, particularly because from bulbs come all those really early, brave forerunners, by many weeks, of spring. Last year I ordered a huge quantity, intending to cram the garden with them. When they arrived, it was blustery and cold and I spent a horrible couple of afternoons on my knees, with a trowel and my nose too close to the soil, my hands throbbing and smarting, as I worked. I loathed those little wrinkled, warty brown bulbs and there were a very great many of them, and they were all very small. (The only flowers I care for which come from big bulbs are lilies.) But one of the eternal laws of gardening is that suffering and labour are rewarded, and from January until April we had a succession of flowers when everything else was black and bare and depressing; tiny, delicate iris reticulata, with their spotted, recurving tongues, in darkest purple and an amazing, Cambridge blue; a special, creamy early crocus, and another, the colour of sea-lavender, tiny narcissi, two or three inches high, with fragile, nodding heads and names like Angel's Tears and Hooped Petticoat, blue drifts of Grecian wind flowers, anemone apennina, scilla, tritelia. I clustered the bulbs anywhere, between shrubs, in the grass, under the fruit trees, and when they came up, they were perfect, it was one of the most successful gardening jobs I have ever done.

The other joys of the winter garden for me are holly, jasmine, and bonfires. Barley village is rich in holly, a tree and bush which is becoming rarer. I think it must have been fashionable up till the Second World War; then, older trees died and were cut down, but people did not re-plant automatically, perhaps because all high hedges surrounding houses have declined in popularity in our open-plan world, of smaller, close-together houses. It's a pity. I love holly for the polish on its dark, dark leaves, and the brightness of its berries, and for its associations with Christmas, and in legend and story. Variegated holly is here and there in the gardens of the village, and that is now even rarer than the green, but I am fondest of the plain cousin. The churchyard of St. Nicholas has three monolithic holly trees whose great bushy heads are pruned every year around Advent Sunday, and the branches fall over into the road and those not taken on a cart to be sold are soon snapped up. It is so expensive to buy miserably small bunches almost devoid of berries, in the town shops before Christmas, that anyone planting a holly bush now with an eye to the future would be providing their heirs with a decent annual income, as well as ensuring the survival of the tree for posterity, and it is particularly nice to be able to invite friends to come and have their pick as a gift.

Winter-flowering jasmine tumbles in untidy cascades over walls and fences and for much of the year it is rather dull and hard to restrain, like a head of wild hair that springs out in all directions. But from the end of November until February, according to weather and variety, it more than pays its rent with all those flowers clustered the length of the thin branches, like blossom stuck into a bridesmaid's pigtail, golden as the sunshine and lovely to bring into the house in sprays, mixed with some simple greenery.

And, to crown it all with another glory, there are the garden bonfires that light and warm us through all the dark days, small ones, built in ten minutes and lasting scarcely any longer, or great, banked-up, Saturday afternoon bonfires that roar and crackle like dragons and can be kept in for a whole weekend with care and skill and the right weather and which finally smoulder more and more slowly, and putter out in a soft sigh of ash. Our garden bonfires are the real heart of winter.

THE BLOSSOM opens slowly, slowly on the apple tree. One day, the boughs are grey, though with the swellings of the leaves to come visible if you look closely. The next day and the next, here and there, a speck of white, and then a sprinkling, as though someone has thrown a handful of confetti up into the air and let it fall, anyhow, over the branches.

The weather is grey, it is cold still. The blossom looks like snow against the sky. And then, one morning, there *is* snow, snow at the very end of April, five or six inches of it, after a terrible stormy night, and rising from it, and set against the snow-filled sky, the little tree is puffed out with its blossom, a crazy sight, like some surrealist painting, and all around us, in every other garden, there is the white apple and the pink cherry blossom, thick as cream, in a winter landscape.

And another day, just before the blossom withers and shrinks back into the fast opening leaves, there is the softest of spring mornings, at last it is touched by the early sun, and the apple tree looks as it should look, if the world went aright, in springtime.

*

In every season, but in spring most of all, the best time of day to be out is in the very early morning. We have had so many cold springs, in recent years, so much late frost, and even hail and sleet, battering down the April blossom, so many gales tearing at the branches as the young leaves are in their first, pale flush of yellow-green; birds have begun to nest and had their nests torn from under them, and even hatched a first brood, only to see them perish over a weekend of renewed cold. April has come and gone, May, which can be the most perfect of all months, has crept in miserably, while we still light fires and draw the curtains early, still wear winter woollens and despair of the early seedlings coming through the cold stone ground. People talk of how summers used to be, in their childhood, long and hot and golden. But I notice that it is the springs that are no longer what they were.

Yet, even in the most dismal, disappointing year, there are days, rare and precious, coming in ones and twos, days that are to be seized at once and relished in every detail, stored away like a preserve, to light us through the succeeding dreariness. There is no time to turn over in bed and say 'tomorrow' and sleep again, this early morning of a fine spring day will never return. Besides, even in a poor year, it may be glorious day in, day out, from dawn until breakfast time, and then the clouds will thicken and the rain return, just as, at the end of these dark afternoons, there is often sunshine and a clear blue sky, a calm bright end to a blustery day.

This morning, the fifteenth of May, I am woken, just after four, by the first sunlight on my face and the singing of all the birds of Oxfordshire in my ears, that dawn chorus begun by the blackbird at the first paling in the sky over Hope-on-the-Slope, and taken up within seconds by the rest. Up the lane, in the long house that lies at right angles to the church, the bantam cockerel is crowing from the top of his midden heap.

I pull the pillow over my head. Four o'clock will not do.

But at half past five, I get up, slip out and set off with my bicycle in the glorious morning, up through the empty village, for on the bicycle, I can see over the tops of hedges and look down the rides, towards copse and meadow and all the flat Fen, I can go further than on foot through the lanes, getting off whenever I like, to lean on a gate or poke in a ditch, and I love the quiet, silky sound of the tyres on the tarmac road, the click of the chain and the whir of the pedals, like wings, when I go fast.

But I walk up the lane towards the church, for the ways out of Barley are steep and hard on the pedal-pusher.

No one is up, save a black cat coming home, mouse in mouth. Most of the cottages which still have thatch wear nets, like hairnets draped over wigs and pinned down tight, against the burrowings and nestings of birds. But the house martins will find crannies and crevices in the angles of roofs and under eaves, there seem to be dozens of pairs flying in and out, and of swallows, too, going into the garage of Ant Cottage, and also into the old wooden shelter that stands at the corner of the lanes; it is rather attractive below the waist, as it were, loaf-shaped and with old wooden legs, a bit like an open barn, though no one ever shelters there or stores anything, it simply stands, on a patch of rough grass and nettles. But the roof is an eyesore, corrugated sheet metal, gone rusty, nailed on anyhow. Not even ivy has grown over to cover the ugliness. But the same pair of swallows come back five thousand miles, year after year, to rear two, or even three, broods under it, and this morning, they are going mad, apparently repairing and re-building, ready for the first batch. Migration, and this sort of regular return across so many thousands of miles of sea, is the sort of common, mind-boggling fact of nature which seems more incredible the more we find out about exactly what happens, but I often wonder what the country people of hundreds of years ago thought; not many of them can have had any idea about what happened to all those birds that appeared in their villages in March or April, and were gone again at the end of every summer. Did they speculate, or guess accurately, or have folk-tales to account for it?

Around and above the church tower are the swifts, soaring high and circling and diving, screaming all the time. They never rest, never alight. When we lived in Stratford-upon-Avon, the arrival of the swifts, which come in huge |numbers into the town, and their departure during the first week of August, put inverted commas around the summer.

Past the gate leading to Cuckoo Farm, and the dog runs out, barks once, runs back busily, and there, they are long up and getting ready for milking, and the yard is full of hens and ducks and geese, running free among the tractors and wagons, the way all farmyards were in my childhood. Paul Plum runs that most old-fashioned and uneconomic of businesses, the small, mixed farm, with his fields scattered around the village, in every direction. He works, virtually single-handed, with a shorthorn dairy herd as his central prop, but also, some corn, grazing fields on the North slopes overlooking the Fen for some beef cattle, and a hundred sheep; he rears turkeys and geese for Christmas, and his sideline is bees, two dozen hives which produce good, plain honey.

From the milking parlour, the clank of the buckets, the chink of the chains, and then the hum as the machinery starts up. Somewhere inside, Paul Plum is whistling.

Round the next corner, alongside Mrs Sleeply's garden wall. Hers is a dull, red brick house, nothing to look at, but her garden is a delight from one end of the year to the other, because it has a bit of everything, and things appear in their season. It would win a prize for the most traditional country garden for miles around. The snowdrops and aconites come up in the grass under the trees, and then the same trees blossom; the laburnum hangs yellow and the ceanothus turns a marvellous, hazy blue on the west wall, there is lilac, both white and purple. There are always sweet-smelling bushes, too, mock orange-blossom, and honeysuckle, stocks and tobacco plants and mignonette, there are rose beds and the cottage border, tall at the back with delphiniums and hollyhocks and sunflowers, low at the front, with bachelor buttons and tiny marigolds. And in autumn, the mighty apple tree, just beside the gate, bows right over the road, so that last year, when the crop was so heavy, before her grandson could arrive with his ladder to pick them for her, Mrs Sleeply's pippins were dropping on to the heads of dogs and children and rolling roundly down the lane.

Now, there is a pencil-line of smoke from her chimney, for these mornings are chill. But I have still seen no one. Bedroom curtains, flowery and frilled, are still drawn at every window.

Once out beyond the last house, I can ride and look over the top of the hawthorn hedge down to the valley below, on the west side of the Fen, where a mist is still hanging about in the hollows. This is one of the best views, softer and more wooded than the one from Moon Cottage, where there is so much space and sky, so much flatness. Here, I see more gentle slopes, meadows dotted with clumps of trees, a line of seven oaks across one field, like ladies in hooped skirts, and as the road bends round by the bluebell clearing a beech copse, whose leaves are just out and still show all the light through them, palest greeny-yellow.

There is a story I heard about fifteen miles away from here, into the Chilterns, that the beech leaves always unfurl on the night of May 5, and I have proved that to be so once or twice. Certainly they come out during that first week of May, and the hawthorn blossom a little later, around the thirteenth. It is out now, though not yet full, every hedgerow as far as I can see has a tide-line of white beginning to spread and thicken. The smell of hawthorn, indescribable, unmistakable, musky and pungent, is Proustian for me, if I close my eyes and breathe it in, I am hurled back to childhood, when I hid under a particular hawthorn tree whose branches bent almost to the ground and sat on the dark, needle-covered soil and pretended to be a gypsy's child.

By the gate to the bluebell copse, I stop, just as Stanley stops the car at the end of every day when he reaches this point, and gets out to look and to smell, while the ground is a sea of that magical blue, and the scent is so fresh, under the encircling trees. Last year, Mrs Miggs was taken out in a car, took tea at the Rectory in the next village, and they stopped here, to give her a sight of the bluebells, and she wept for joy, though her eyes are so dim, now. But she could distinguish the blueness, and smell the flowers, and she said it was exactly the same as she knew it more than eighty years ago. She has spent all her life in the same cottage in Barley. She had never thought that the bluebell copse would still be there, never dreamed of seeing it again.

I have memories of bluebells, perhaps everyone who has lived in the country has them; mine are of walking through Raincliffe Woods near Scarborough with bluebells all around me and stretching away, like another ocean, of bluebells up to my middle, of lying down in them and of pulling them up by their sappy stems until my fingers were wet and green, unable to learn the repeated lesson that they would not last, would droop and wilt so sadly long before home. There is no sadder sight than armfuls of bluebells thrown into the ditch and left to rot because someone has felt cheated and not even bothered to get them home.

The bluebell wood is also the rabbit wood, here it is that the baby rabbits scatter madly out of holes in hedge and ditch, down the bank and across the road, every time we pass by, in spring, and here, inevitably, however careful we are, once or twice we hit them, and then hope we have hit them hard enough, so that they are not left crawling in pain along the hedge bottom and into the long grass to die slowly.

One or other of us, often both, comes down these three miles of country lane, every day of the year, to work, to school, to shop, and then there are these occasional slow bicycle rides, we know every inch of it, and have noticed how it is punctuated by the haunt of a different bird or animal at various clearly-defined points.

So, in this copse, we see rabbits, usually only in the springtime, but then, every day. Now, there must be rabbits all over this area of countryside, in every foot of field and ditch, copse and hedgerow, but it is only here, just here, that they emerge regularly for us to see; neither of us has ever had one run before us at any other point on the journey home.

Nor have I ever seen a jay, apart from here, in this corner by the crossroads and the cottage-in-the-wood, but sometimes – and, again, more often than not it is in spring – there is that wonderful gaudy flash of feather, and the raucous cry.

In front of the little cottage-in-the-wood there are wallflowers, growing all around against the stone walls, in lines up the path, packed close together as pins, in the way they look best, and it is another of those flower scents full of nostalgia, this time for my first school, where wallflowers grew under the classroom windows, I remember the smell of them, borne in on the breeze, it goes with the smell of chalk and ink powder and wooden floors.

As I ride quietly down the slope beyond the crossroads, a pair of green woodpeckers swoop away ahead of me and into the trees, but they are not alarmed, as they so often are when I surprise them in the garden of Moon Cottage. Probably, they are not aware of me here, at all, and neither is the fox, who stands just beside a farm gate on the sharp bend, though his ears are pricked, he is tense as an arrow held in a taut bow. His coat and bush are the rich red brown of chestnuts, and it is the chestnut trees that I see now, over the top of the hedge, though the cow parsley here is in full flower and high as my shoulder, I haven't a very clear view. The White House, opposite a short scree of Douglas firs, has a great many horse-chestnut trees surrounding it, which is surprising, for I always think of them as town trees, the trees of every suburban avenue. Now, their candles are blazing, mostly white, a few red, their leaves large as outspread, giant's hands.

I wonder when they will bring the tractor and the mechanical scythe along and cut down the verges which are so thick and luxuriant, after such a wet early spring, and a great danger to drivers on all these blind bends. Perhaps never, because of the County Council's lack of money, and we shall enjoy all the wildness, and learn to drive with one elbow resting on the horn.

I stop and get off, climb on a gate and look over it, and away down acres of sheep field that slope steeply towards the last, flat acres of meadow before the main road, a mile away. Here, it is quite quiet, the sun is getting up a little, warming my back, there are dewdrops trembling on the spider-webs that are draped over the wooden gate, and a thistle is glinting with moisture. Here, there is no sound, no sign of human life at all. Down there, beyond the sheep and their lambs, what gleams silver is metal, the roofs and mirrors of cars and lorries, silent, because what breeze there is is blowing in the other direction, taking the rumble of the engines away from me. But, when the wind blows uphill, and especially when the trees are bare between, you know, just here, that you are on the very edge of the city, and all the pastoral remoteness is an illusion.

And there, five miles off and beautiful against the sky, are the dreaming spires, ethereal, glittering, insubstantial in the pearly, misty air of this early spring morning, and I cannot mind them, if that were all of the city I should welcome it.

I turn around, get on the bicycle again and see what I expect to see, just here, a yellowhammer, and then another and another, flitting about and in front of me across the road, for this is the point where we always see them, there must be dozens of nests within a few yards. Why just here, why, apparently, only here? In autumn, you see flocks of goldfinches at the same point, but then it is easy to discover why, they come to feed on the thistle heads that grow in a clump of waste ground near the fir trees. Well, there may be something similarly attractive to nesting yellowhammers.

As I ride back, the first flush of birdsong has faded a little, as some warmth comes into the climbing sun, and the sky and the air become clearer, the larks begin to rise and, as they rise, to sing; and there is no song like it for concentrated joy without pause. I often see them like this on top of the ridge above High Holt, and much earlier in the year, too, in March, when there are often some wonderfully clear days. I look up until I can see them no longer, they seem to melt into the upper atmosphere, though the song remains, falling down like fine rain. I used to see them like this in Suffolk, on the marsh path beside that metallic sheet of river just outside Aldeburgh, where sky and water merge as they meet and there seems to be no land. Out there, where the sound of the sea drops behind you and it is oddly hushed, is the best place I have ever known not to see but to hear birds, curlew and redshank and even bittern sometimes, or the beating of a swan's wings, like wooden clappers as it flies overhead; and the larks, always the larks.

As I ride back, I still see no one, and the meadows around me are yellow as butter, with buttercups and with marsh marigolds down where the streams run beside the willows, and with cowslips, too, for this sort of old grazing land is the last haunt of those increasingly rare flowers, though we seem to have a good number each year. There is a field that rises up from the back of Nance and George's cottage which is as thick with cowslips as if they were common daisies or clover.

Back at the bluebell clearing, I stop again, leave the bicycle leaning, climb the fence.

Under the trees, it is cool, still, filled with a greenish light coming through the young leaves. It is like swimming undersea. Seconds ago, all the branches above were alive with birds, nesting, feeding, singing, excavating for insects among the dead bark and leaves of the woodland floor. Now it is suddenly silent, there might be no other living thing here, and there is a wariness and a fear in the air, like a sort of electricity. Among bluebells and bracken, on an old tree stump, I sit down and wait, scarcely breathing. The moss of the bark is damp as a mole's pelt to my touch, the air smells sweet and musty.

Nothing.

From the village, the church clock strikes the half-hour.

Still nothing.

I am looking at a branch of pale leaves and silvery bark and then I am staring straight into the eyes of a grey squirrel. How long has it been there, stiff and still and watchful, its grey the grey of the tree trunk?

Pretty things. Pretty, from yards away, but not close to, for then you see the yellow teeth and probing snout of the rat that it really is, nothing but a rat with a wonderful, upcurving, bushy tail, a scavenger, a menace. It darts away, and begins to leap from branch to branch, graceful, sure-footed as a monkey in the jungle.

And then the song starts up again, one by one the birds have begun to move, through the little copse, going about the earnest business of parenthood, but still warily, not showing themselves.

I stand up and go quickly, trying to disturb them again as little as I can. The smell of the broken and crushed bluebell stems rises up from under my feet, for there are so many, I cannot help but tread on some.

I meant no harm at all, going into that clearing, to sit for a few moments in the early morning, but back at the gate I feel like a vandal.

At the farm, the cows are standing in the yard waiting for the last few to finish being milked and then to be sent back to their pasture, there is the hiss of the hose on concrete. The dog rushes out again and barks once, and then back, and here and there down the lane curtains are drawn, a milk bottle gleams on a stone step.

But, in Moon Cottage, they are still asleep. I let myself in quietly and make a pot of tea, and take it outside, to sit under the apple tree and feel pleased. In the Buttercup field, one of the newest calves, born a couple of nights ago, feeds and nuzzles and then wanders a yard or two away from its mother. It is white as milk, huge-eyed. The wrens are flying in and out of the woodshed and the bluetits in and out of a hole in the wall, by some guttering. Over the fields and farms and rooftops of Barley, the sun climbs and climbs. The dew has almost dried. The best of the day is done.

Creatures

THE BUTTERCUP field that lies just below Moon Cottage is a classic English meadow, permanent grazing for cattle over many centuries, like so many similar fields around Barley. They are too exposed for crops and too marshy for the plough, because of the streams coursing below, which make the ground waterlogged on the lower slopes. But these fields are fine for cattle, which go into the Buttercup field on the first of May.

A week before that, on a fine spring evening, as soon as Stanley came home from work, we all put on wellingtons and went for a walk in the meadows. We were really hoping to see the baby hares. Almost every morning in March, I had looked out across this field, and the Rise that leads up from it, to see hares behaving in that legendary way, going mad, racing about in circles, the males boxing one another to impress the females. Sometimes, they were lying in their forms, pressed close to the ground, and so still, so well camouflaged, we could not be certain they *were* there, until we looked through the binoculars and saw the gleam of those great watery eyes, the black ear-tips.

It is, somehow, always a surprise to see animals behave as they do in stories and proverbs.

The field was full, not only of buttercups and cowslips, but of that pretty plant of the wet meadows, lady's smock, which is a delicate, mauve colour. But, otherwise, all was yellow, for spring *is* yellow, from the first, powdery pale catkins on the trees, in February, to the dandelions, yellowest of all.

At the bottom of the slope, the stream was running over some stones, very clear and shallow, sandy at the bottom. Jessica splashed up and down and then stood on an old plank that someone had thrown across to form a narrow bridge, and rocked it to and fro, and then, at last, ran, up the slope through all the flowers, laughing and laughing.

We turned left, began to climb a stile between the hawthorn hedges, and froze on top. In the great field below us, that stretches right down to Fen Farm, and is mainly grazed by sheep, were the hares, dozens of them, with parties of leverets, racing about, playing, feeding on the young grass, and the early evening sunlight kept catching their pale fur in bands.

We watched and watched, and then one of us moved a foot, or made some other, slight noise. One hare stopped dead, then another, sat on hind legs, ears pricked and quivering, and then, in all directions, they ran, incredibly fast, the young following, making desperate little squeals, and in seconds they were gone, the field was entirely empty and still.

Then, from the copse, the cuckoo started up, the cuckoo that I first heard on April 17, but who then went silent again for the week of late storms and snow. Now, he was in full voice, his inane, annoying cry repeated and repeated all day from various clumps of trees and the hedges of the wilder gardens. It is the very sound of May, just as the hawthorn is the smell. You can't like it and, if it lasted throughout the year, you might easily go mad, it is an unattractive bird to look at – though hard to see – and its habits are downright nasty. But its voice is one of the landmarks of the season, and it is the herald of better things to come, and so we welcome it. We have a friend, an Anglophile America city-dweller in his eighties, whose main ambition, now, is to hear a cuckoo call, for he never has, and perhaps he never will, for he is rather deaf. But, if he came and sat under the magic apple tree for an afternoon in May, it would be quiet enough, and then he might listen to the cuckoo-cuckoo-cuckoo until he had his fill.

*

Not so many villages have ponds now as once upon a time, but Barley has a pond, at the top of Fen Lane, a pond raised up a couple of feet from the road, so that you climb up on to a grassy bank to stand beside it, and above is another bank, steeper, overgrown with trees and shrubs and grasses. Down this bank trickles the water from up on the ridge, and into the pond at one end, and out, splashily, by a stone runnel, and down into the drain in the road at the other, so that there is the never-ending, pleasant sound of water.

It is an oblong pond, and often, in spring and summer, the surface gets covered with a dense, creeping mat of bright green algae, obscuring the water and the fish beneath, and it has to be dragged off with long, hooked canes.

There are newts here, and water beetles and dragonfly, all kinds of skimming insects and crawling, underwater molluscs, and best of all, in early spring, the frogspawn. The children of the village catch it in nets and put it into jam-jars and take it home, to transfer it to bowls and buckets, hoping to breed their own frogs. One enterprising small boy of eight sold his spawn at ten pence a jar, to a girl even shrewder, who then sold her frogs at ten pence each. As she reared several dozen, this represented a rich return on her investment. At the end of May, I bought Stanley a small garden pond of his own, as a birthday present. He sent for water lilies and oxygenating plants and snails, bought six goldfish, arranged the whole most beautifully, with a couple of stones for effect, and plenty of gravel at the bottom. But what was missing, he said, were frogs. Too late to get any spawn, he bought some of the enterprising Olivia's. They were exquisite, not as long as my little finger, and the most subtle, olivy-willowy green, with legs so fine they might have been made of hair. They swam and they sunned themselves on the protruding stones for the whole of one Sunday, and in the morning they were gone, taken, I suspect, for tasty morsels by the magpies. But the mortality among frogs is grotesque; of the millions that reach their full development from spawn, relatively few survive, which is why there is still a dearth of them in the countryside.

All around us, in our first spring at Moon Cottage, wild animals and birds were breeding, and in and around the village the farm animals and the dogs and cats bred, too, and Jessica looked at the ten labrador puppies from Church Cottage and the cat Hrothgar's first of two regular annual litters of kittens and at Mrs Plum's newly-hatched silky bantams, and the milk-white calf in the Buttercup field, and said at last, 'But we only have an old, old cat and some hens whose eggs don't get babies,' and so, by choice and chance, we began to extend the family. One of the white hens went broody, and was borrowed by my neighbour Lavender to sit on a dozen fertile eggs, which she did most efficiently, and proved an excellent mother. We visited her a good deal.

In the beginning, there was the cat Hastings, mine for sixteen years, fat, somnolent, partially blind, touchy. She had not taken kindly to the arrival of husband and daughter, and grew introspective and resentful, but, worst of all in Jessica's view, she was neutered. And so we acquired Polly. Polly was a London-born kitten, orphaned at three weeks, when her exquisitely elegant mother Herodia was killed by a car, and reared by human hand, together with her two brothers, so that she came to us another three weeks later, more used to people than usual. She was very small, with hair that stuck out in all directions like a sooty halo. For a week, the older cat ignored her, in a puzzled sort of way, perhaps scarcely able to see her, and Polly clung close to us. Then, one morning, she was off, like a ball of fire, jumping on Hastings from the tops of tables and chairs and window-ledges, chasing her tail and swinging on it, teasing her, biting and mewling, and the old cat stirred and began to rumble like a smouldering volcano, and then, late one night, erupted. It took a month for the fires to die down, and even now, though Polly is calmer and wiser, she sometimes feels provocative, there is a skirmish and a shower of sparks.

We got Polly so that Polly would get kittens, at least for a year or two, for there is no more delightful way of instructing a child about the way all creatures mate and give birth and suckle and mother their young, and of teaching her tenderness and respect and responsibility towards all living things.

The village husband to every un-neutered female cat is Charlie Sleeply, a battle-scarred monster, half-wild, altogether fierce, whom no one has ever been able to catch to have spayed, and perhaps they haven't tried too hard, for it would surely be wrong to submit that fullblooded tom of all toms to such an indignity and humiliation. But Charlie Sleeply has lots of wives, and Polly is not the nearest, so perhaps it will be some time before she presents us with kittens.

What finally put paid to the sparring of the Moon Cottage cats was not sense or maturity or any chastisement but, simply, the arrival of a dog, which united them in (temporary) feline outrage.

No dogs, I had always said, and I would still never keep a dog if we lived in the town, nor ever have a puppy, either, I find puppies tiresomely destructive, fawning, puddling creatures. The only dogs I care for are work dogs, and dogs that know their place, dogs that behave, and are treated like dogs and dogs alone.

For two years, Jessica had an imaginary dog called Tree Trunk. He was my ideal, invisible and silent. There was *one* dog, though: a scruffy little, brown-faced terrier belonging to old Miss Reevers, in the last cottage down the lane. He used to peer out between her net curtains if one went by, and trotted up the lane past Moon Cottage once every day, on a lonely outing. I liked his face. That, I said, is the only sort of dog I would have, if I were ever to have a dog at all.

Then, Miss Reevers was ill, and died, and the dog, whose name was Tinker, needed a home. Within a week, he had his feet under our table and a place in all our hearts. I was right about him, he is the perfect dog, quick-witted, cheerful, willing and grateful and moderately obedient. He looks like every small boy's terrier, small and wiry and spry. He chased the cats up the apple tree until he realised how strongly we disapproved, and now, although he gives every other cat in Barley a run for its life, ours he leaves alone, in spite of their provocations. He is affectionate but not sloppy, anxious to please, a good companion on a walk, and he retains a streak of purest independence. He is what Moon Cottage needed all along.

What Stanley had always wanted was a tortoise, so Theodore came in a box for his birthday, and clears up all the dandelions and buttercups, as well as the bolted lettuces. He roves freely about, and it is quite impossible for him to get out. If the cats, the dog or a hen, go near him, he hisses like a serpent as he withdraws into his shell, but he is responsive to humans, probing out his leathery neck to be scratched, and when he spent a morning in Jessica's nursery school, during Pets Week, he was equally sociable.

When the six goldfish were put into the newly-established pond, they fled under one of the stones and didn't come out for days. I despaired of their ever moving gracefully, calmly about the water in formation, for us to enjoy, and still, whenever our shadows fall suddenly across the surface of the pond, they are inclined to vanish. Polly sits on the edge and stares at them and dabs a paw, and is angry with the water for being wet, tantalised by those flickering shapes, but in the end she stalks away and washes herself, sleek and supercilious. And even the old cat Hastings emerges, now, no matter whether the dog is in the garden or not, and sits on the stones beneath the apple tree, while a white hen and a brown scratch contentedly side by side among the marigolds, so that for a while, in the spring sunshine, we have a very peaceable kingdom.

Food

S PRING MEANS Easter means eggs. Real eggs, eggs warm from under the hen, and a hen who ranges about freely and contentedly in a large area of garden, grubbing up greenstuff and worms, scratching vigorously, making a bowl in the earth for her dust bath, and settling there, before retreating once a day to the soft, dark, hay-lined nesting box in the hen house and taking her time over laying her egg.

It sounds very romantic. It is perfectly practical and possible. We do not have a vast acreage, but we built a hen-run of thirty feet by ten in a dull patch of weedy ground below one of the stone boundary walls, put in a new hen house, bought six White Leghorns and, later, four Rhode Island Reds and off we went. They are the minimum of trouble, and work, and it is not at all necessary to let them out into the garden, because they have ample space in their run, and in spring, when there are so many vegetable seedlings about, they stay put inside their wire. But, once everything is rooted and established, they do little harm, and they are more contented when allowed to scratch in the undergrowth and rubbish beneath the plum tree at the back of the garden. Free-range birds are busy birds, without time to be aggressive and peck at each other, or eat the eggs, and the absolutely fresh, free-range egg is simply a different species from the stale, or even fishy-tasting (not to mention cruelly-produced) battery variety. Once upon a time, everyone who had a bit of back garden, in country or town, kept a few chickens, and it is a pity there are so many bye-laws forbidding it in residential areas now. They are only anti-social if a cockerel is kept within earshot, or the hen-run is not tended properly, and allowed to smell and attract vermin.

In the spring, as the days lengthen, the hens give of their best; we generally have one egg per hen per day. I sell a few and we eat a great many, and these fresh eggs are best of all simply boiled or poached or scrambled, rather than used in baking or elaborate dishes. I like omelettes. Ever since I was given my small, cast-iron, non-stick omelette pan, I have found them very easy to make – the quickest, tastiest meal available.

By the time the hens are laying well, the first herbs are shooting through again in Stanley's herb garden, the tarragon, which over-winters indoors, in its pot, chives outside the kitchen door, parsley, and – nicest of any with eggs, easy as pie to grow – the pretty, ferny chervil. Any of these, chopped, make a delicious omelette aux fines herbes.

Because there is always spinach in the kitchen garden, except in April, when the old plants have gone to seed and the new are not yet established, we often have eggs Florentine – poached eggs, or oeufs mollets, on a bed of spinach. I steam the spinach for a few minutes, chop it, reheat it with butter, salt and black pepper, put the eggs in hollows on the top, and pour a light cheese sauce (Cheddar or Gruyère) over the lot, and brown it under the grill.

Shrove Tuesday is not in spring, of course, but we have home-made pancakes on other days, too, piles of very thin ones, with lemon juice and with treacle, with honey; and then there are eggs in little pots (in thin cream, flavoured with tarragon, topped with cheese, put in the oven until set).

Most people in the country make some use of wild food – 'food for free' – and, in the autumn, the lanes are full of blackberry-pickers. Rose-hips and elderberries and crab-apples are made into jelly and syrups, sloes into gin, green walnuts, if you are lucky enough to find them, are pickled, and mushrooms are much sought after for delicious breakfasts. Otherwise, the idea of gathering and cooking some of the other edible but not very delectable plants and berries has too much of the playing-at-gypsy image about it for my liking. I don't actually see myself boiling samphire, candying primrose flowers or stuffing dock-leaves. But two wild plants that are very easy to find in early spring, and well worth the effort too, are sorrel and nettles.

Young sorrel leaves are not unlike spinach, but they have a delicate lemon flavour. You can make sorrel soup (one pint chicken or vegetable stock, cook the sorrel leaves in a little butter gently for ten minutes or less, make a roux, stir in the heated stock, simmer a bit, add the sorrel, liquidize the lot. Season and add a little thin cream or top of the milk if you like). A sorrel purée is good with fish, and sorrel and young spinach leaves, chopped up, make a good salad with crispy bits of fried bacon added and a good French dressing

Nettles are suitable for eating during only a couple of weeks of the year, before the plants have grown tall and the leaves coarse. They have to be picked with caution, and probably with gloves on, unless you have very hardened fingertips, and then only the topmost four tender leaves. They are nicest made into soup in exactly the same way as the sorrel, though Stanley, who swears by the comfort of *les infusions*, makes nettle tea, and sweetens it with honey. He also makes mixed herb tea, mint tea and camomile tea, all of which look, smell and taste, to me, unutterably disgusting.

In May, there is asparagus. When we lived in Stratford-upon-Avon, we were on the edge of the Vale of Evesham, a rich asparagus-growing area, and got it in quantity, early and late (though not necessarily cheap), both the large sticks and the thinnings known as sprue. I have now established an asparagus bed of my own, using two-year-old crowns of the large Evesham strain, but we shall not be eating any of it for another year, and not in abundance for another two or three. Patience is the requirement of asparagus-growing. Until, with luck, we have plenty of our own, we shall only eat it a few times each season, and eat it *au naturel*, steamed and buttered. But its flavour is the very flavour of late spring, and it will be worth the waiting for an abundance.

Whether you are picking your first early potatoes in late spring or early summer depends on the variety and when you planted the tubers, and whether or not you were caught out by a late frost. I am cautious about putting mine out until the second week in April, so I can rarely lift anything worth having until mid-June, but there is one way of getting a few pounds in May, and that is to grow two or three seed potatoes in a bucket indoors, in a mixture of soil, sand and peat. It's a hit or miss business. You have to bring them into the light the moment they begin to show through the soil surface, and not let them get either too waterlogged or too dry, and you may end up with a few marbles, or nothing at all. But it is worth a try. Once, just once, we had about seven pounds of plum-sized beauties, the skin flaked off as you touched them, they needed cooking for only about seven minutes, and they tasted earthy and fresh and wonderful, with butter and a lot of parsley.

Until I got a steamer, I was always depressed about rhubarb. (By a steamer, I don't mean anything at all expensive or elaborate, but an aluminium pan with holes in the bottom and handles at the sides and a lid that sits on top of any sized saucepan, full of boiling water, and cooks all your vegetables in a short time, retaining all the flavour and colour and vitamins and not letting them go soggy, as they do when in actual contact with the water.)

When we arrived at Moon Cottage, in among the jungle of growth that was to become the kitchen garden, we found two or three crowns of old rhubarb. When the plot was rotavated, the rhubarb went under, and no great loss either, thought I, but it didn't mind the treatment a bit, only came up and divided and multiplied like some biblical tribe. Now, Jessica has gigantic green umbrellas for her dolls, and the tortoise and the kitten get lost in the dark, cool shade, and it all looks rather handsome and branchy. But what to do with the fruit? I used to cook it in little or no water and it went mushy and dull-looking, and then I tried baking it in the oven, and it dried and shrivelled, and no one in this house likes rhubarb jam, even when flavoured the way a Swedish friend showed me, with a vanilla pod. I used to look at all those young, thin, bright pink sticks turning into odd, tough tree trunks in despair. Then, I tried steaming the stuff, and the result was perfection, chunks of rose-tinted, cooked but absolutely firm, shapely rhubarb. I have thrown out all the recipes for mush, for fools and jams and whips and sponge-toppings, and now we have the still-warm fruit, sprinkled with a lot of demerara sugar and covered in clotted cream. I also like it with thick, goat-milk yoghurt, which I get, until I can find a way of keeping two goats myself, from the Bruins at Scattercotes. It is also good flavoured with snippets of orange or lemon rind, and you can put a vanilla pod in the steamer, as well as in the jam.

I have read all sorts of amazing stuff in the gardening books about how you have to replenish the crowns of rhubarb and put pots over it to force it and blanch it to keep it tender. Rubbish. If you get one crown, you can divide it each year and it will take over the garden, and the way to get rhubarb tender is simply to pick it young and keep picking it. It will, like most plants, oblige you with more and more and more, throughout the spring and summer.

Spring is lambing time, the fields are full of them, bleating and leaping, frisking in pairs and trios, playing the way all young things play, and Jessica says how lucky the farmers are to have all those lambs to play with, just as we have our cats and dog, and I say, yes, yes, and then the first, milk-fed legs of lamb are hung in the butcher's stalls in the city market, covered in that creamy white caul that looks so like a baby's lacy vest, and it will be tender and delicious, served with the earliest of the potatoes, the very first, tiny broad beans and carrot thinnings, and I cannot bear it, for the meat tastes of mother's milk and sweet meadow flowers, and turns to ashes in my mouth. I rush off and cook a great mountain of vegetables and an egg or two and that will do for supper. I can still look the sheep on Common Down in the face. But, later in the year, I shall manage the chops all right, thickly smeared with my own mint or redcurrant jelly, just as I feed our own hens in the morning and then go to collect a freshly-killed one later the same day, from Forest Farm, at Hope, to eat that night. I am, as Stanley says, a sentimental, non-practising vegetarian. But, if I were obliged to eat no meat at all for the rest of my life, it would, on the whole, be a relief and no hardship.

75

Produce

As with winter, so with spring, the gardening writers are disarmingly optimistic. If you read enough of them and then measure your own progress, you will feel guilty and depressed, and spend hours wondering just where you could have gone wrong. In March, they say, when the days are beginning to lengthen, and the ground to warm up a little, and when you have dug and manured and composted every inch of your ground the previous autumn and winter, busy yourself from dawn to dusk making your first sowings of beans, peas, carrots, lettuce, potatoes, establishing your seed beds and digging your trenches for runner beans and celery. By April, you will be hoeing between all those long, straight rows for sturdy green shoots, which will by now be several inches high.

But, in Barley, March is invariably still winter – and Barley is not, after all, in the North of England. Gales rage, rains lash down, or else we are under several feet of snow. The ground is cold as stone. If you *do* get a couple of mild days, and are foolish enough to sow early peas or French and broad beans, they will lie dormant for weeks, or else rot. If they do come up, there will be severe frosts waiting to pounce on tender tops, over Easter, and pinch and shrivel and blacken them.

In my experience, you rarely gain anything by sowing too early but, instead, lose rather heavily, in both seeds and labour. Nature usually makes up for itself at the other end of the year, so that we often get long, warm autumn stretches in October and even beyond, when vegetables that should have been long over are still flourishing and being picked and eaten.

Mr Elder, a good, old-fashioned country gardener, was in hospital last spring, for almost six weeks, and when he was fit enough to be out and doing again in his garden it was May. Even I had sown most things by then and they were coming on well enough, whilst his plot still looked bare and brown. In a couple of days, in his quiet, unhurried, steady way, born of seventy-odd years' practice, he had accomplished more than takes me a couple of weeks, and by the end of June his crops were further forward than mine. My beans and peas had simply been sitting in the cold soil waiting to germinate when the sun eventually shone, his went straight into the nicely warmed-up ground and came through within days.

After seeing that, I stopped fretting every March, as I stood watching the birds splash about in the puddles of the vegetable plot, or waded about in the snow to pull the last of the leeks.

If we have a mild spring in future, all well and good; if not, I shall sow in May and June, and still end up with plenty.

Plenty of what? When we first came to Moon Cottage, I planned to grow plenty of everything. After my initial experience of clay soil, of the temperamental nature of some crops and the amount and variety of attention required by others, I became more modest in my ambitions, and tailored them to suit our own particular needs and tastes. Above all, I had been misled yet again by those books, and by the sight of other people's kitchen gardens, and memories of all the country gardens of my childhood. The books assume that you will grow everything, and the allotments were always crammed with rows of the traditional English vegetables. But there are quite a few things that none of us likes at all. The day I realised that there was no natural law which said that I *must* have beetroot, parsnips, radishes or sprouts, and that there would be no serious loss of face involved in admitting that carrots simply would not grow in my garden, and that I could buy maincrop onions far superior to any I could ever grow, was a day of liberation indeed.

So it was that, our second spring in Moon Cottage, I made a kitchen garden plan. I would grow only what I thought I could successfully grow here, with luck and good management, though the odd, new experiment each year would be permitted, and I would grow only what we like to eat and, most of all, what is infinitely better home-grown and fresh-picked just before cooking. In the space saved by not attempting all the other things, I would grow what we did want in larger quantities, in succession, and in several varieties.

My list read, in no particular order, new potatoes, peas, mange-tout peas, broad beans, French beans, runner beans, courgettes, spinach, celeriac, leeks, sprouts, broccoli, very early turnips (Jersey navets), asparagus, globe artichokes, lettuce, shallots, Florence fennel. I had a separate fruit list, but the chances of doing well with almost any soft fruit in the exposed garden of Moon Cottage were slight, and for the time being I put this on one side.

No sooner had I made my list and drawn up a plan, than another truth dawned. I did not have anything like enough ground. I could, for a little while, behave like an aggressive nation, and make raids on to the flowerbed and lawn territories of the garden, claim them for my own by digging them over and planting vegetables, but that would not go on for long, simply because of the dearth of possible areas. We do need some grass, for Jessica's slide and paddling pool, and for general games, and as a passage-way from one side of the garden to the other. Besides, Stanley draws the line at looking out from the sitting-room window on to rows of beans, peas and potatoes. I cannot at all understand why, myself, I would as soon look at them as at most flowers, and in any case I grow sweet williams and tall daisies in nice rows, for cutting, between the vegetables, and edible peas have flowers every bit as pretty as sweet peas. We could always train a honeysuckle up the chicken run. But I was driven back by the herbaceous border lobby, though not before I managed to secrete two rows of autumn-fruiting raspberries behind the delphiniums and surround the pond and the patch in front of the woodshed with courgette plants. I had a ninety per cent success rate with two packets of seeds, dozens of strong, healthy plants, and we like courgettes very much. Besides, their pumpkin-coloured, blousy flowers go on and on for months and are as handsome as anything in the posh part of the garden.

I crammed every inch of my space full but it was still not enough and, besides, I had other problems. You cannot grow anything remotely tender and shy in the garden of our cottage, or anything that rises above three feet and requires a lot of staking, because of the winds. Mange-touts, and runner beans, which go up to six feet and beyond, were out, so were the tender artichokes, and the French beans, which do not like this heavy, cold clay. I could not give over the huge areas that the permanent crops of asparagus, artichokes and strawberries need, *and* grow all the other vegetables as well. There seemed to be no way out. Meanwhile, once the worst of the spring storms were over, I was working half the day and well into every evening, re-sowing all the beans and peas which had rotted in the wet, or been taken by the jackdaws which nest in two of the cottage chimneys every year. This year, I had netted every row with tunnels of chicken wire. It looks ugly, and is unpleasant and hard stuff to work with, but the main drawback was that, like cloches, it was pulled out of the ground by high winds at least three times during the night, and at dawn, before I could mend matters, the birds had eaten their fill. Peas and beans are hard work. They like deeply-dug, well-composted soil (what doesn't), so there is a lot of back-breaking ground preparation and, because we are only a low stone wall away from the cow pasture, we have a lot of tough perennial weeds, dandelions, buttercups, bindweed, couch grass, ground elder, which have to be uprooted. Trenches have to be dug and well-trodden down, and then there is the sowing (more back-bending) and the netting, and then the re-sowing, either altogether, or in patches; twigs, hazel preferably, have to be sought out and cut, and driven into the ground, as stakes – or, failing twigs, canes and netting. But they are nothing like so efficient, or so pretty.

I grow Little Marvel and Feltham First, and three tall rows of Carouby de Maussane mange-touts, those most delectable of all peas, whose young, flat pods are picked when small, steamed quickly, and eaten whole, with butter. Anything with the words 'dwarf' or 'bush' attached to it gets an automatic trial in Moon

79

Cottage kitchen garden, and most French beans are low-growing. But I find them horribly neurotic; they hate the cold, in the air or in the soil, refuse to germinate for the slightest of reasons, then refuse to flower, or crop sparsely, or wilt suddenly, when six inches high, for no discernible reason, or collapse on to the ground after heavy rain, or in strong winds. They are delicious, but I was about to give them up in despair, and the mange-touts and the runners, too, because I was sick of hearing them all crash to the ground, staking canes, wires and all, and hauling up the mass of greenery to its feet, like a recalcitrant tent, the next morning.

Potatoes may be hard work, too, in the planting-out and earthing-up stages, but after that they are no trouble, and they don't seem to mind much what sort of soil they grow in, nor how hard it rains, or blows, though they are vulnerable to late frosts, if the shoots are not properly covered over. The joys of having one's own new potatoes are worth any amount of sweat, and we had a tremendous crop in our first year, from eight rows of tubers, with no failures at all, though one whole section began to turn yellow and then brown about the leaves, from some nutritional deficiency, but it did not affect the potatoes themselves at all.

Lettuces I do in succession throughout the spring and early summer, from a packet of mixed varieties, including Cos and Webbs and Butterhead kinds, and, although I try to sow them thinly, I never thin the seedlings themselves out at all until they are quite big, and as dense as parsley. Then I use half a dozen at once, when they are in young, tender leaf. Whenever I have thinned them early – a dreadful job, in any case – and let them grow to full, individual heartiness, lettuces in this garden have come on too slowly, and become tough, snail- and greenfly-ridden, and inedible.

By May, everything was sown and sprouting, I had a plot reserved for the celeriac and broccoli plants, and even bought two ugly and costly growing bags, to line up along the path and supplement the space. But, one Sunday, I stood and looked at things. 'What I need,' I said, to the evening air, 'is another garden.' An allotment, said my husband. Yes, but allotments are in the town. I even began to wonder if I wouldn't be better off back there. I love allotments. I like all those makeshift sheds with old bits of guttering propped up to drain into rain butts, all those old gentlemen in braces and white shirts and caps, smoking pipes, chatting, tying huge cabbages on to the handlebars of ancient bicycles. You can tell the seasons by all the runner bean wigwams and sweet-pea frames, the gaunt rows of sprouts and the marrows on manure heaps.

Failing an allotment, I wondered if anyone in Barley, particularly an older person, might have a garden that they were finding too much for them to cope with alone, and might let off a piece of it to me. So I went to see Mr Albert Baker. The Bakers live in Fen Cottage across the lane from us. Bakers have been in Barley for generations. Albert's father was the Rector here, and lived in the Grange when it was the Rectory, Albert's mother started the school and an orphanage for girls. Bakers used to own a lot of the land around, and Albert still does have some, which he lets out for grazing and hay-cutting. He knows everyone in the village, he is a tremendous gardener. His wife, like my husband, does the flowers, while he, like me, does the vegetables. I have learned a very great deal simply from looking at Albert Baker's kitchen garden, and from watching him at work, and talking to him about this and that. I thought that, if I told him I needed an extra plot of good ground, he might come up with an idea. But what he came up with was better than my wildest dreams. 'Why don't you have,' he said, 'a piece of my old orchard?' and pointed across the field behind his house.

The orchard is huge and rectangular and has a view down rolling pasture land, towards Lyke Wood, and then away across the western area of the Fen, and the village of Idle, beside the river in the far distance. It is bounded on two sides by hazel coppice, on one by a hawthorn hedge, and, at the far end of it, stands Lyke Wood House, whose garden and orchard it has always been. But all the old apple and pear and plum trees have had their day and been cut down, the house is divided into flats, and the garden is too big for anyone to cope with, and Albert has quite enough as it is. So it has been wild, full of nettles. Sad.

We walked over there, and stood among the few remaining pear trees and the last of the blossom, looking away to the south and west. On the other side of the road, in the garden of Moon Cottage, there was a chill wind blowing. Here, it was several degrees warmer, sheltered and balmy. The nettles were waist-high and still growing, but Albert shoved a few aside, and dug at the ground with the toe of his boot, to reveal a patch of soil. It was like soft, brown sugar, a rich, sandy brown loam, full of the humus of years of fruit tree leaves and flowers, and then the nettles, composted down gradually, naturally.

'You'd grow anything here,' Albert said.

'Anything.' I was imagining it. 'How much can I have?'

'Much as you like. As much as you can clear.'

'How much rent do you want for it?'

'I don't want any rent. I want to see the land used.'

'Done.'

It was one of the best bargains of my life. The following day, I marked out as large an area as I thought I could reasonably cope with, plus a bit more, and the next week two young men with machines came up from Chalford and cleared the nettles and rotavated the ground and pulled out old tree stumps and roots, then removed all the debris. They left a beautiful, clear piece of ground, allotment-sized. I went to gaze with shining eyes, and make plans.

It is a lovely place in which to work, in between the trees, quiet and sheltered, bird-filled, windless. There is a very small pear tree in the centre of my plot, to lean on, and rest and look out over that mellow, ample view, which is gentler, with softer outlines, than the view from Moon Cottage. The blackbirds and thrushes and warblers were nesting all around me that first springtime, the blossom fell and the new leaves flushed out, and I raked and dug and marked out and sowed, in that crumbly soil, and it was such easy, pleasant work after the cottage garden.

And how things grew! French beans, the variety called dwarf

burgundy, with their grape-coloured flowers and wine-dark pods; they came up without protest within days, burgeoned and flowered; the runner beans climbed to the top of their eight-foot frame and tipped over again, the mange-touts flowered profusely, and everything was pollinated by the masses of bees that always seem to be about the orchard.

I sectioned off a large asparagus bed, and another for globe artichokes (the variety Gros Vert de Lâon), put purple- and white-sprouting broccoli and spring turnips in the seed bed, and another two rows of lettuce, and made a border of sweet williams, from plants someone gave me.

The nettles came up again, weakly, and I chopped at them, and they died. The bindweed did not and, almost every day, I rooted up a yard or so of it, and took it away to burn, but it will be a long time before I eradicate it completely. A rich soil for the vegetables is also a rich soil for weeds.

There have been one or two other teething troubles in the orchard, and I had to spray with a far stronger pesticide than I generally care to use, to control red spider mite and a bad invasion of blackfly. Water is not on tap, but I bought a rain butt, and carry buckets and cans across the field every time I go, understanding, as I do it, the lot of peasant women centuries ago in England, the women in the Third World today. Fortunately, soon after I planted the artichoke suckers, which must not dry out until they are properly established, the wet spring weeks began, and later on we had sunshine in time to encourage the pollinating bees.

The extra work is more than worthwhile. It would be worth twice as much again, for the walk across the sloping field, where the four, great sycamores stand sentinel, spreading, full, and through the wicket gate, into the old orchard, for the sight of everything growing so strongly and profusely, and for the peace of the place, best of all in the early morning, or at the end of the day. But it is quiet at all times, a sanctuary for the birds, the butterflies, and bees, for the growing plants, and for me.

It was a good spring.

People

I N THE spring, bit by bit, day by day, as the nights lengthen and the weather brightens, and as the gardens are sown and planted, the village comes to obvious life again, and people come out into the open, like animals from their winter retreats. There may be dark days still, especially in early April, and there is more rain and cold and greyness, too, as the winter drags itself slowly away over the hill. But there are some fresh, clear mornings, with the dew on the grass, and balmy breezes on which the smells of grass and freshly-turned soil come, and in May there is real warmth in the sun and all things burgeoning.

Then, all those friendships are renewed between people who may not have seen one another for a good deal of the winter, because they are too elderly or infirm to go walking out, or are not members of the choir or the whist club, the Young Wives' Thursday afternoon group or the Women's Institute.

People walk their dogs without being too brisk about it now, and take a stroll to the pub, and do their gardens, or else simply stand, in the doorway that lets on to the lane, at the gate, by the wall, watching to see who goes by, giving good day, catching up on the news. Mrs Miggs takes her upright chair, with the old, round knitted cushion and her crochet, and sits in the porch, and Mr Harrow, who is very old, very lame, opens his window wide and sits at it hour after hour, and the canary sits beside him in its cage. It is light walking up to the W.I., and light to cycle up to Scattercotes, to get some goat cheese from the Bruins.

I go across the lane to talk to Albert Baker, and ask his advice about sowing peas; does he firm the trench before, and the soil on top of the sowing after, or only one and which? and to take the eggs that Jane buys twice a week, and Jessica comes with me, skipping and hopping from side to side like one of the young lambs up the lane.

'This is spring,' she says, 'this is spring *now*,' to Mr Harrow, and she picks a bunch of dandelions for Mrs Miggs, who sits with the rug over her knees, and the flowers lie on it like gold doubloons. The close proximity, in a small village like Barley, of the very young and the very old, is a fine thing, especially for a child like ours, who does not have grandparents to hand. Small children will talk to anyone, once the guard of shyness has fallen, and they have, like the elderly, a sense of immediacy, a need to say or do something, now, now, the minute it is thought of, combined with that other sense, of the complete irrelevance of time.

Mrs Miggs was married sixty-two years ago, in Barley Church, from the Grange where she was then in service, and where she met her husband to be, who was one of the gardeners, and they went back there for a year or two, until her mother died and it was her job to return home, a hundred yards away, to the cottage she had been born in. There, she looked after her father and her husband and, later, her dead sister's three children. The Miggses had, as she put it, 'no cuttings' themselves. She remembered the dances at The Grange, every Christmas, and Midsummer, for all those in service in the house, and the rest of the village, and the balls for the carriage folk, and the parties for the girls from the orphanage. She remembered when Moon Cottage was three cottages, each one up and one down, with as many as eight people living there.

'There was never so many houses then,' she said, 'but there was a good few more people.' Barley was a large village once. It had two shops, a cobbler, the inn, a butcher, a baker (who only stopped baking five years ago and is still living in one of the almshouses). There was the mixed school and the orphanage and a Men's Evening Institute, and a Methodist chapel as well as St Nicholas Church, and each place of worship had two choirs. Mrs Miggs lent me a bound volume of Parish Magazines of ninety and a hundred years ago, and there, among the records of baptisms and marriages and burials, were some of the names of our present neighbours, Elder and Miggs, Harrow and Ash, Baker and Plum and Dove. It is surprising how many people we know who are old Barley people and their fathers and grandfathers before them, and many of them still live in the same cottages, though they are greatly enlarged and modernised now. And there are young generations, too, grandchildren who work in the city, unless they are farmers, but who still live in Barley, and great-grand-children at the village school.

On the corner of Fen Lane and the slope that leads up to High Holt and the Ridge, there is a house called the Old Forge, and the farrier, Mr Dove, still occupies it, though it is no longer a forge in the strict sense, for his forge is his van, he is a travelling blacksmith, as they mostly are nowadays. His son John is a blacksmith, too, and last Easter Monday John Dove got married in Barley Church. We went to look on, of course, standing by the lynch gate with half the village, and it was a sunny day and a pretty wedding, but even better was the ceremony outside the Old Forge, before all the guests went over to the Carpenter's Arms for the reception, when they Fired the Anvil. It is not a Barley tradition. Blacksmiths all over the country have had an anvil fired at their weddings for generations and many still do.

There is no lawn in front of the Old Forge, just a couple of narrow flower beds, but opposite the cottage is a low, grassy mound, on to which the anvil had been dragged. Everyone stood around it, all over the lane, and there were two big fireworks stuffed into the anvil hollows, with a makeshift fuse, a piece of tape, leading down on to the grass and across the road. A lot of fussing about, and checking and re-arranging, a lot of family cameras to the ready, and then the farrier and his new wife were pushed forward a little, and the farrier's father lit the fuse. It crept slowly, slowly, towards the fireworks. The children began to get restless, everyone looked either embarrassed or worried, or a bit cold, in the spring breeze, but expectant. Two blackbirds were singing like mad in the lilac tree above the bank, and just as someone was saying, 'It's gone out,' there was one bang, a puff of yellow smoke, and then the second, bigger bang, and everybody cheered and applauded and clapped the farrier on the back and kissed his bride, and the blackbirds flew off, screeching, startled, into the trees. The blacksmith was well and truly married.

Jessica and I strolled back, past the pond, and up the High Street, back to the church, and climbed the steep, gravelled path between the leaning gravestones to the ancient wooden door. There were daisies growing like confetti in the grass. From here, you can look over the higgledy-piggledy thatch and slate and stone of all the rooftops of Church Lane to the blue line of hills that lie on the far side of the Fen. There were little scraps of white cloud, like trails of lamb's fleece across the blue, and birds again, singing everywhere, birds in the bushes and trees and on fences and gateposts, plain, everyday birds, thrushes and wrens and dunnocks and robins, singing for spring.

We went inside the church and the air still seethed quietly with the wedding that was just over, it was warm with all the breaths of the people and sweet with flowers and scent. We stood very still by the altar, looking at a great vase of white and yellow narcissi and apple blossom and I felt the imprint of this marriage service somehow sinking gently down and down on to us and being imprinted on to the fabric of the church itself, into the stone of the walls and the brass of the rails and the stained glass of the windows, being absorbed into the ancient building as everything before it had been so absorbed, every hymn and anthem and voluntary, every blessing and vow, every petitionary prayer, every praise in the morning and thanksgiving at evening, every bidding of welcome to a child and of farewell to a dead soul.

The church was empty apart from my daughter and me, and it was not empty at all. She felt it, too. She wandered quietly about, touching this and that, talking a little to herself.

We closed the great door carefully, let down the latch, in case a bird would get in and be trapped.

Outside, there were white and pink paper petals on the ground, and spring sunshine.

That Easter Monday evening, Mrs Miggs, in her ninety-sixth year, rolled up her crochet, and took in her chair, at the end of the afternoon, and closed her door and went to bed, early, as she always did, in the room that used to be the parlour, for she had not been able to climb the stairs since breaking her hip five years before, and in the night, in her sleep, died.

And so there was a funeral service at the church to follow the farrier's wedding, and people in Barley felt saddened, for Mrs Miggs was so well-known and liked, such a familiar figure, she had seemed immortal, and another link with the old days, the old village life, was severed. Sad too, we said, that she did not reach her hundredth year, to which she was looking forward. There would have been a party for her and the children would have made posies and taken them, and sung to her outside her window in the early morning.

But a good funeral service, at the peaceful end of a long life, is not altogether an occasion for mourning. This one felt fitting, and things were in their proper order.

Mrs Miggs' cottage is up for sale now, and it will have to be renovated and perhaps altered drastically, and never look the same, and we miss the sight of her, on her chair with her crochet, as we go up the lane past her door, of an evening.

*

Many is the tale of woe I have heard about people who moved into the country, got 'a bit of land' and were bent on self-sufficiency and organic gardening, the good life. They acquired chickens and a pig and some goats – always goats – bees and perhaps a spinning wheel, dug up an acre for vegetables and, sooner or later, came to grief.

So I have been very wary of the siren voices. They said, 'a bit more land to grow more vegetables' and I listened and they said 'hens' and I listened, and acquired both, but then I turned the

sound down on the voices. Our way of life is too busy, too complicated and finely balanced between various activities to allow for
those animals whose daily care is such a tie and a responsibility,
over and above the ones we already have. We need to go out or
away, separately or together, we are both working at jobs outside
the village, we are not committed to the ideal of providing
everything for ourselves. But the sirens kept on saying 'goats', so I
thought the least I could do was to look into the whole subject of
their keeping. I knew in advance that they would be no good for us
at all. Twice-daily milking all round the year would be far too much
for me to let myself in for; we do not have either enough land, or the
right sort of land, for goats do not particularly like grass; Stanley
does not drink any milk at all, and two goats (you have to have two,
or they pine) would provide far too much for Jessica and me, even if
I made a lot of cheese.

All the same, I went up to see the Bruins.

The Bruins are both in their twenties, and struggling, in a
dilapidated, rented cottage-plus-couple-of-acres, to be truly and
completely self-sufficient. They make pots and they paint, and Nell
does woven pictures; they have enthusiasm and starry-eyed ideals,
and two young children and no money and the water is fast closing
over their heads. They will have to give in, I know it. They are cold
in winter, and she is weary and worn-down, and the children are
constantly ill. No one buys their work, or not much, and their
animals get sick, because they do not really have enough expertise
to cope with them, nor can they afford to pay a vet's bills.

Yet I am on their side, because their ideals are right and good, in
spite of being ill-thought-out and impractical, and because they are
so happy together, and so kind and gentle. Their house is a mess, a
homely, scruffy, impecunious mess, but they have reclaimed an
unpromising field, and made things grow. They have rotten luck.
Their first seed potatoes were given to them, and all diseased; they
tried to sell their produce at the gate, but no one knows they are
there, so there is no passing trade and everyone in the village itself
already grows their own. When they put up signs on the main road,

a man from the Council came and told them they were trading illegally, so they took their produce into the city markets, and there they continue to sell it, but the traders take a large profit from them first. They staggered from season to season, and now think they might try and acquire a caravan and become gypsies, or a canal boat, and become water gypsies.

What they do know about, though, are goats, or at least Nell does, and she sells the milk to quite a few customers in Barley, and her own goat cheese, too, which is salty and creamy, tangy and crumbly and altogether delicious.

She has six goats now, so there are always kids about the place. They graze both the meadow, the orchard and some scrubland which a farmer lets them use in return for cheese, and make a pretty sight, and a pretty sound, too, because Nell has put bells on the woven collars round their necks, so that it sounds like Switzerland, near to their house.

By the time I had spent an hour with her, I had confirmed my feeling that I wanted to keep goats very much indeed, and that I could not possibly do so. Not yet. So we shall just go and visit Nell's and buy their milk and cheese. As long as the Bruins are up there, that is, but they seemed very depressed about their prospects, although quite firm in their commitment to a country life, to self-employment and self-sufficiency. But I suspect that, to make it work, you have to be both larger, in terms of the amount of land and animals you have, and more ruthless and efficient and blinkered than Nell and Rod are or could ever become, and, also, rather more professional about what paperwork has to be done and cannot be evaded, and better at producing pots and paintings than either of them, with their modest talents.

A lot of people derided the Bruins when they arrived, and a lot of people would gloat if they threw in the sponge, but I should be sorry, and for the village, too, because they bring the right spirit to us, unacquisitive, loving, relaxed, the opposite of time-serving, and they have a contentment and a stillness, in spite of their troubles, which makes their company so refreshing.

Moon Cottage

B Y THE springtime, Moon Cottage was beginning to settle
down around us; we were finding out its strengths and weak
points, and now the whole place fiitted together around our
daily lives. We had done the initial, very necessary work of repairing
and renovating, and we had done the interior painting and wall-
papering. It was all suiting us perfectly.

But, one morning in that first spring, I opened all the windows,
and saw how peeling and shabby was the paintwork on doors and
ledges, and how ugly, in particular, the concrete wall overlooking
the garden and the fields, now that we had removed two old,
overgrown trees, a lilac and a laburnum. I went into the bathroom
one morning, too, and although it was bright and sunny outside,
this was dark and gloomy. Jessica's room, with its three, outside
walls, had been terribly cold all winter, and it stands over Mr
Elder's storeroom, so that there is no warmth rising from below,
either.

So that was three jobs, three lump sums of money spoken
for – the outside painting, including that wall, a window to be cut
out of the sloping ceiling of the bathroom, and cladding and
insulating for Jessica's room, re-plastering, and laying a new,
well-insulated floor there, too. In addition, the roof over the boiler
room, which had looked doubtful from the beginning, was now
looking just a little worse. We are not, either of us, capable of any
household jobs of a modest kind, let alone this sort of work, and I
began to feel depressed, to believe that we should never have taken
on an old house, in which something is always going to need
patching and mending and propping up, however basically sound

the structure. I was going to have to try and earn a bit more money.

There was something else that had been preoccupying me, and not until Mr Thomas, our excellent painter, came and whitewashed that ugly, bare wall outside, had I been able to see a way forward. What I lacked in Moon Cottage was a room of my own. There are two bedrooms, and Stanley has the third as a study, doubling as a spare room. I had been sharing it, but our books and papers were muddling hopelessly together.

I do not require a large or a grand room, but I have always had one in which to work, to close the door on everyone and be myself. In winter, I had eventually taken to writing in the kitchen and, later, to having my desk and papers and typewriter on the small, light landing, which is a little room in itself, albeit a passageway too, and overlooks Mr Elder's greenhouse, and the lane up to the village. That, and the kitchen, are fine when no one else is in the house, but they will not do otherwise, and moreover they are not really mine, not private places.

The wall was whitewashed. I stood looking at it with pleasure, for it had transformed that side of the house; I like white paint, almost anywhere at all. I also admired the extent and quality of the view I got, both near at hand, and far away, when I stood with the wall at my back. Just in front are a small flowerbed and a few straggling herbs, and then a stretch of grass, down to the stone boundary wall. Then it came to me. What this wall was standing waiting for was a conservatory, the kind the Victorians had, lean-to, with white-painted brick up to waist level, and ornamental mouldings and gutterings. If I could have that, with a door at one end of it and an electricity supply for heat, a well-insulated, tiled floor, then I should have my room, private, inaccessible from the house, a room in which to work and sit and look out and think, and also where I could try to grow a fig and a vine, and have a lemon tree and some lilies in pots, I would put a bench along one side, for bringing on a few early beans and lettuces and other tender plants (though this was not going to be in any sense a greenhouse), and a desk-height table, running all the rest of the way round, for working at. A sloping roof, with slatted, bamboo shades, and careful ventilation everywhere, and all would be well in every season.

I telephoned an architect friend, and a week later she arrived, saw the wall and began to measure up and draw sketches, as excited by the possibilities as I was.

I have been in love with conservatories since my childhood, when we lived in a Victorian-built town by the sea, where every other house had one, octagonal or rectangular, ornate or merely functional, though many were falling apart, and had had their glass removed or blown out, during the last war. I loved the smell inside them, earthy, musty, close, secret. The smell of geraniums anywhere reminds me of conservatories. There were some huge, public ones, hothouses where fountains fell into dark green pools, tropical plants with amazing, surrealistic flowers climbed up, and parrots flew about among the leaves, and those smelled even better, damp, steamy, jungaloid.

I love the look of conservatories, the play of light within them, the reflections through their glass, the effect of greenery and flowers against white woodwork. In mine, I want to have white-painted Edwardian wickerwork furniture and a bamboo screen, and pretty white china jardinières, warm terracotta flower pots. Such a room of my own, with such a view over the countryside, is the stuff of dreams. But, at Moon Cottage, my dreams were beginning to take on substance, to emerge clear and three-dimensional, real and tangible, like towers and turrets revealed through the parting of cloud and mist.

I was anxious that the design and construction of my conservatory room should be entirely sensitive to the rest of the cottage, for to a certain extent I was wanting to impose an alien structure, a twentieth-century-made, nineteenth-century design on a mid-eighteenth-century dwelling. Outside, as well as in, it is easy to mix and marry styles, but you do have to do it cautiously, even while following your instincts about what will look right. There is nothing so stuffy and boring as the room where every single item is in period, in the same style, it has no individuality, it might have come from a museum or a film-set. And the same is true of a house, too, especially one like Moon Cottage, which has undergone so many changes. But one false move, one vulgarity, one step too far, and everything is ruined.

The plans were drawn up slowly and adjusted time and again, I went to stand and look at the white wall and try to see this or that feature in my mind's eye, when imposed upon it. But the spring fever for creating my room was running very high, and I knew in my bones that it would be right and that Moon Cottage would accept and accommodate its careful addition without resentment.

Festivals

N̶O ONE keeps up the old traditions any more, they say, everybody is far too busy . . . people don't go to church nowadays . . . you couldn't tell the difference between the seasons if it weren't for the trees.

But it isn't true. Come to Barley, go to any village anywhere in the country and you will find people marking the seasons by the traditional feasts and festivals, and not only the popular, commercial ones of Christmas and Easter either. Nor is it any self-conscious attempt on the part of a few who have a desire to turn the clock back. Those people may dig about in local record offices and archives, and come up with all manner of country customs which were once upon a time regularly repeated, a natural part of the rural community life, and then try to whip up enthusiasm to revive the events artificially. For a year or two, perhaps, they succeed, but it is all contrived, all applied like a patch, not woven in as part of the fabric of everyday life. When the enthusiast dies or moves away or directs the enthusiasm ëlsewhere, and fails to continue applying pressure on the rest, the custom slips out of sight again, as dead as it ever was before. Those that survive must do so by universal wish and natural practice, or not at all.

Well-dressing has survived in some parts of the country, and so has pace-egg rolling, mainly in the north of England, but that loveliest of all customs, the dressing of the graves in the churchyard with white and yellow flowers, for Easter Day, so that when it dawns there is a glorious, visible symbol of the Resurrection, that is no longer kept up. I wish I had been alive to see it a century ago, as Francis Kilvert recorded it in his diary of country life, when people of every age and all social classes and occupations went with their flowers up to the churchyard, because it was the regular and right-seeming thing to do, as it still is to exchange Christmas cards. Then, every family had relatives buried in the village churchyard, generations of them usually, and it was where they themselves would end; the population was not so mobile, local roots were more permanent, and there were no crematoriums.

There are some people in Barley today with family graves in the churchyard of St Nicholas and, on Easter Saturday and Sunday, fresh flowers, all the flowers of spring, are placed on the stones and the grass around, as well as in the church itself. We have a rota of flower ladies, all of them with well-stocked gardens, so that, for all but the darkest, barest days of the year, the vases and jugs and urns are filled with the everyday, seasonal flowers that are available for picking. When there are few flowers, there are leaves and berries and branches.

No one makes any formal 'arrangements', nothing of tortured shape and unnatural stiffness, no jarring juxtapositions incorporating chicken wire and stones which are in certain places thought 'artistic'. Flowers are massed as in the best, crowded borders, the colours and shapes simple and harmonious and seasonal.

On Easter Day, all is fresh and free, there are daffodils and pale blue and mauve irises, tulips and forsythia, butter-yellow primulas and spiky sprays of broom, every window sill and ledge and alcove is full of flowers, and there are circlets of them around the font and the base of the lectern, like bridesmaids' coronets. And the church of St Nicholas is nothing if not traditional in its celebrations and so, just as, without fail at Harvest time, 'We Plough the Fields and Scatter', on Easter Day we sing the resurrection hymn and at Whitsuntide 'Come Holy Ghost our hearts inspire'. And so I like it, so it should be, as long as repetition of what has always been said and sung is not all, and the spirit of each festival is re-created every year, to give it renewed meaning.

Lent begins when it is still hard winter, but Mothering Sunday, whatever the actual weather, creeps into the beginning of spring on the calendar, and in Barley there is one ancient custom kept alive, the girdling of the 'mother church'.

This year, the day was grey and blustery, and the wind was blowing off the Fen, too, so it was very cold, it made our eyes water, climbing the steep path that leads to the church, and inside the heaters were on full, it was hard to believe it was really spring, at least until the children went up the aisle in ones and twos and collected a posy of flowers each from the great flat basket carried by the Rector, and came back to present them to their mothers.

Mine was made of primroses set in a little pincushion of velvet moss and, when I bent my head to smell it, the smell was damp and earthy at first, but then, it came through, the delicate, unmistakable scent of spring on the soft yellow petals.

There was a baptism in the middle of the service, too, when farmer Paul Plum's latest son was christened Nicholas, like the church, and he cried lustily and his mother and grandmother and godmother wore spring hats wreathed in flowers, so that, while we were all still inside the building, we could believe in the season.

It was harder when we all went out to watch the children hold hands and girdle the church, in their pretty dresses and Sunday suits, walking round the grass path – and it is a long way round – and singing, in the wild wind which was now bearing rain on its breath. But there were primroses nestling in the grass beneath the gravestones, and on the top of the lych gate a thrush began to sing, its feathers ruffled, as we made our way down the lane to home fires and hot drinks.

On May Day morning even the thrush was frozen silent and the rain poured coldly down from dawn. In Oxford city, choristers sang on the top of Magdalen College tower and revellers made merry in the streets below and a poor time they had of it. In Barley, there was to have been the crowning of the May Queen in the school garden, and her procession, with all her attendants, around the village on the back of a decorated farm cart, and it had to be cancelled. We stayed indoors all day with the fire piled high.

Oh, treacherous spring!

I AM AWAKENED, a little after dawn, by silence. It is the very end of July, the time when no birds sing.

I go out into the garden. Six chimes from the church clock. Already, it is hot. I has been a close, still night, for once; even up here, no movement of air stirred the curtains.

I stand under the apple tree. The blossom has all gone. The fruits will not come until later. Summer is the time of leaves. The shade of the little tree, like a parasol inverted over my head, is a dark, even green, there are no changes in the light as the leaves move.

Last summer, because of old age or some deficiency or disease or neglect, many of the leaves of the apple tree were eaten away at the edges, or else had large holes in them, it was a poor sight, and I wondered if it was coming to the end of its life. But I dug about below to loosen the soil, scattered a handful or two of general fertiliser and forked it lightly in. How it was appreciated, how well the tree seems now! Every leaf is firm and glossy and even, and there are far more of them, and none has a hole. It is as lush as any fruit tree in the prime of its life.

From its shade, I look over the Buttercup field, down to the stream, the willows beside it, and the Rise beyond. All the cows are clustered near the water, with just one or two grazing a few yards further off, and it is so utterly quiet, so still, that I can hear the soft slap of their lips around the grass, the tearing of it out of the ground, and then their jaws, munching, munching.

In the distance, all the trees of Fen Lane and up on the opposite slope are dense and heavy and dark green as the apple tree, there are only slight variations in the shadings between them, and they look flat, like cut-out trees in a picture book.

The branches are empty for most of the day now, the birds do not come at this time of year.

The apple tree is pausing, resting through the hot days. At noon and for about an hour of the early afternoon, it is the only shady place in Moon Cottage garden, the only place under which you can sit comfortably. We are very glad of it.

Life in Summer

SUMMER DID come at last and, when it did, it was one of those summers of poems and stories and country pictures, a once-upon-a-time summer, it was hot day after day, week after week, so that we slipped into a dream, where we imagined it never ending, a paradise world of long, golden days. Time stretched out into the pale far distance and the mists that girdled the day about, so that we seemed to be somehow suspended, floating in them. When we awoke, it was to a soft, pearly mist, like a gauze, that left the faintest veil of damp on skin and hair, and on the grass and the leaves and the wooden fences. Then, the sun came striking through within minutes, the mist had cleared, it was as though the Fen absorbed it, breathed it back into itself, and like a brilliantly lit, brightly-coloured stage everything was suddenly revealed, there were rooftops and chimneys and white gates and yellow stone walls, there were the church tower and the chestnut horses in the Dove-house field and a red tractor and trailer, they all seemed strangely artificial, as though they had been very carefully placed in position just a moment or two before.

Then the day grew hotter, and duller, the gleam went, everything seemed to be dusty and heavy, even though there were no clouds at all, the air was oppressive because of the lack of any breeze, the stock-stillness of it meant that you seemed to be re-breathing the same stale patch in and out, in and out.

Tempers of children frayed, farmers, their backs brown as wal-nuts and wearing canvas hats, worked in the fields, bringing in the late hay, dogs lay about under hedges panting wetly, and in the air, the faint, over-all smell of decay, a seeping uncleanness hanging about in corners and oozing out of ditches, lingering on the nostrils, the smell of hot countryside without rain for weeks, when streams dry up and all the dung-heaps and drains and cesspit outlets bake in the sun.

The other smell is of dust, dust from the hedgerows as cars sweep by, dust from the lanes when horses stir it up, dust from the last dry hay being cut and tossed and baled, and the beginning of the corn harvest. It is sneezing weather, and itching weather, there are insects everywhere, clouds of thrips, the tiny black thunder flies that descend on sweaty flesh and stick, and bite, midges that tangle with your hair and raise lumps, gnats that jazz above the surface of the pond or the water butt, fleas that hop over your feet and on to your legs from the grass, cattle-flies, horse-flies.

The evenings are the best part of the hot, dusty, glaring days, still, close, calm, before the Fen exhales the mist again and the distant hills are blotted out, and then all the fields, beyond the nearest few, everything is shrouded in mist. But it is a different mist now, yellowish, then pinkish, rather than white, and dry, not dewy. Later on, after dark, it will be just a little cooler.

Yes, a hot summer. But, although it seems to have had no beginning, to reach back as far as we can remember, that is an illusion born of heat and dust and cloudlessness. Summer began late, after a poor spring, for all there were a couple of weeks of flowers and freshness, spring was a disappointment, nothing much more than a backlash of winter, as though the cold season had a long, long tail that trailed slowly away behind it. It was a grey, wet spring, dismal and cold, and even the first ten days of June were fires- and lights-on-early days. The first flush of roses came out on walls and around doorways and porches, New Dawn, Albertine, Gloire de Dijon, Sanders White, all their glory was wasted in rain and scudding skies, and many of them even came down in blustery winds.

On the school playing field, on Sports Day, children were given hot drinks and swaddled in jerseys and track-trousers between races, and parents sat under car rugs. The cover was scarcely taken off the swimming pool, the school garden fête was postponed, and then held indoors, outings were cancelled, picnics abandoned. Cricket and tennis were played under lowering, swollen skies on damp grass, the soil was cold, and all the vegetables and soft fruits were held back, slugs and greenfly multiplied and throve.

And then, over one weekend, it changed utterly, we might have been transported to another country, we were hurtled into the middle of high summer with no reparation, no time to acclimatise ourselves. It rained hard all day on the eleventh of June, and not again for weeks and weeks, the sun bore down and the earth baked, until September.

These, too, are days to begin early. I like to be the first awake, first up, to go outside alone, with bare feet, and look around me, at the mist and the still fields and the trees just visible. I return to the kitchen, open the windows, and make my coffee, feed the dog and the cats. There are no sounds from the village at all. These are the most tranquil mornings imaginable. I let out the hens, who begin to chunter and cackle excitedly the moment they hear the front door open, and scramble out of the pop-hole like so many bullets, towards their food and water. I collect letters and newspaper from the box at the top of the stone steps, and pause there, before I come down again, to look over the apple tree's cascade of leaves to the sky, beginning to clear, so that I can see Miss Jones's donkeys now, through the clearing mist, eating thistles half a mile away.

Some giant crows are circling over the cornfields below. Nothing else at all visible in the way of birds or animals, nothing scuttling or bustling, even as early as this, before it is too hot for them.

I go and poke around the kitchen garden to see what's to pick, what needs weeding and watering most urgently, how much damage the insects are doing, and to notice the bees moving satisfactorily in and out of the pea and bean flowers. Bees are about, even in the hottest weather.

The flower garden is all betwixt and between, with half the border flowers over and flopping, wilting, dying, the rest not yet come out. The roses are between their June and September flowering, but the hollyhocks are climbing to the sky, their washed-out, chintzy-coloured flowers floppy as cotton skirts. Among the vegetables, there is a riot of gaudy marrow and courgette flowers, dozens of them, down among the vast umbrageous leaves, a pleasure for months on end. The pea flowers are white and pink, the strawberries luscious red. Whoever thinks vegetables are mundane to look at?

Down at the bottom of the Buttercup field, the cows are all drinking at the stream, which is still flowing, though slowly now over the stones. The sun is up and striking warm on to my face. From the house behind me I hear voices. The family is up.

We take plates and bowls and mugs, or apples and peaches in the hand, and eat whatever breakfast we have each foraged for in the garden, on the wooden seat beneath the apple tree, sitting on the step, or on the edge of the little pond, watching the first, creamy-petalled water-lilies unfurl, flatten out and gradually reveal their yellow hearts and orange stamens. The petals are in densely-packed layers, like flowers cut out of paper.

The dog Tinker is at my feet, the cats come padding across the grass, to sit and wash themselves thoughtfully. It is a good time, no rush to school, no rush to do anything at all. Jessica finds an 'ant's house' under a stone and gazes and gazes at the seething millions.

By nine o'clock, Stanley has driven off to work, Julie has arrived to look after Jessica for the morning, while I work, the day is under way, and the weather, and the countryside outside the window, shut out of my mind until lunch-time. But I look up, now and again, and see the heat haze shimmering over the cornfields, and that the sky is no longer blue but silvery white, surrounding a great sun. I am working in Stanley's room, where it is cool, but the hens have retreated behind their house, to find some shade, the dog is under the apple tree on the stone slabs and the cats up among its bowery branches. Jessica is in her paddling pool, lying flat on her back.

No one wants any lunch, just drinks, cool drinks, and fruit. I put Jessica on her seat on the back of the bicycle and take her off to a friend's house a couple of miles away, to swim in their big, blue pool and play with her children. Later, I will join them, but for the moment, home, to take a book I must read upstairs into the cool, white bedroom, and lie, read a few lines, and then drift off into a gentle hazy midsummer sleep, an hour, an hour and a half, the hottest part of the day. Through the window come the noises of summer, the grind of the tractors in all the fields round about, a monotonous, soothing sound.

Everyone comes home, and we eat in the kitchen with the doors and windows all open, and still there is no coolness to be found, nor any breath of air. In Jessica's room, under the eaves, the room which is so cold in winter, the temperature is now oven-hot, in spite of the wide-open windows on both sides. She will not be able to sleep until very late. So I leave her, lying on top of the sheet, listening to stories, and go out, to give the dog the walk he has been restless for this past hour.

Sometimes we go through the village, stopping at every other house to chat, while he runs to and fro impatiently. But, tonight, we turn to the right outside Moon Cottage,and down the steep, stony lane between the high hedges. There are deep ditches on either side, with water usually running down, but now they have dried to a trickle at the bottom of the undergrowth of roots and fallen branches and brambles, you have to stand very still and quietly and listen hard before you can hear it at all. Tinker keeps vanishing. He knows every rabbit hole, used and disused, every gap in the fence, every short cut accessible only to dogs. I lose him and he re-appears ahead of me, and pads back and forth, sniffing, stopping to scrabble now and then, lifting his leg, then emerging, to trot away. A dog like this covers at least two miles for every one of mine. He is inquisitive, alert, enjoying himself.

At the bottom of the lane is a stile. I stand on it for a moment, and look ahead. In front of me the hay field drops quite steeply down, and on either side there are similar small fields, divided by good, traditional hedges. Behind me, Paul Plum's tractor chugs across, he is working every evening now until half past nine or ten o'clock, he and his brother from the next farm, and all the farmers around, only leaving the fields when it is too dark to see. They are very late getting in the hay, it was so wet and poor in the spring and early summer. June hay, the sweetest of all, was July hay and early August hay, the cutting of it, in the hot weather, merged into the corn harvest, which the farmers understandably resent, for they like at least a short break in between the two spells of intense work.

But the grass is all cut now and some of it is baled up, the wagons have been crawling like prehistoric monsters up the lane, laden and swaying, every evening. A little is still lying, swathed out on the ground, drying, greenish-gold. At the edges of the fields there are poppies. I have never seen so many as there are again now all around here. When I was a child, the summer countryside was a sea of scarlet poppies, like a French Impressionist picture, and then they were gone, killed off by chemical crop sprayers. Now, because of economies and conscience and greater care, farmers are spraying less, and some, like Paul Plum and his brother, scarcely spray at all, the District Council do not cut the verges so ruthlessly, and all the poppies are back in the hayfields and on the fringes of the corn and in amongst it in places, too, dancing, bright, and free. And there are wild scabious again, of that heavenly blue, I can see a few from here.

Below the hayfields, we are on the flat, the Fen stretches away and the Fen, at the moment, is corn, golden corn as far as I can see and further, miles away into the mist, it is silky and tall, pale as pale, not golden now, at the end of the season and of the day, it has been dried in the weeks of sun to a far more subtle colour. Corn is beautiful. The loss of hedgerow and coppice and individual trees, in the corn prairies of East Anglia and the Wolds, is a dreadful one, yet for a few weeks, the waving wheat, all those open acres of oats and barley, is a glorious sight. Under the full sun, or when a cloud comes and shadows chase one another across the surface, and it changes in the changing light, like the surface of the sea. I am reminded, as I look down, of Thomas Traherne – 'The corn was orient and immortal the wheat.'

But, though the Fen is full of corn, the line of it is broken here and there, by the dykes and the remaining hedgerows, and towards the centre, the wild, marshy tracts of land where nothing is cultivated. And immediately below me, slightly to the left, as I climb the stile and begin to make my way down the hayfield, is Lyke Wood.

It is a small wood, as all the best ones are, for small, in woodland terms, is friendly and safe. It is forests that are terrifying and impersonal, deadening miles of landscape. Small woods like this one, which is triangular in shape, can be walked in and through and out the other side of, can be known, and there is light at the edges, only in the very heart of it is there that oppressive green darkness, in which you glance over your shoulder, sounds are exaggerated and your heartbeats and breathing come a little faster.

But, this evening, I do not venture very far inside. Where I walk, on a brackeny path, the light sifts down between chinks in the foliage and filters through between the trunks, and where saplings and suckers and tall nettles mark the wood's edge. It is a curious light, yellowish, a little blurred.

In May, Lyke Wood is full of bluebells and wild anemones and birds madly singing. In autumn there is the constant shifting and rustling, as the leaves drift down. In winter, squirrels leap away just ahead of you from branch to branch and the whole place is open and pale and bare, to the sky.

But now it is absolutely silent, absolutely still, the only sound I hear is that of my own footsteps and the swish of the branches that the dog pushes through. No birds, no breeze. And no flowers either. This is the dead time of year in a wood. I don't much care for it and the shade is not cooling and refreshing, either, but close and stale, pressing in on me like felt.

I am glad of the dog. I reach the pale golden light rising from all the cornfields around, and step out into it and into the warmth of the evening sun, with relief.

At my back, on the slope, Paul Plum's tractor, busy as an insect. Directly ahead, to the west, the sun is gathering a haze, like the silky white fleece that spins itself round a globular cactus, and the haze spreads out more thinly to the far horizon, I cannot see any of the hills.

The insects are getting under my skin. I whistle to the dog and climb back slowly up the incline, reaching the hayfield and the hedgerows before sitting down on the grass, to chew a straw and scratch Tinker's back and look out over the countryside again. There will be a dozen jobs to do in the garden, but most of them are being left, these hot days and sultry evenings. Fortunately, because it is so dry neither grass nor weeds are growing much.

Sitting with the dog in a hayfield is as good a way of passing this particular time of the summer's day as any I know.

In Sheep Hill, Paul Plum switches off his tractor. A flycatcher darts from its look-out on the fence, darts back again, as though someone has jerked a string.

The air seethes, with heat, and dust, and quietness.

The Garden

I HAVE ALREADY already said that I do not have a great deal to do with flowers in our garden. Vegetables and fruit are my province. I will spend any amount of time and energy on the growing of those. There is a streak of the puritan in me, which chides me that time spent on things which merely flower and possibly smell nice, are merely ornamental, is time frittered away. Nor will I do outdoor housework. There are suburban gardens which look as if someone has taken a vacuum cleaner and a duster to them every day. It also happens that there are rather a lot of flowers and shrubs I actively dislike. But, when summer does come, I always wish I had spent just a little more time the previous autumn and spring in planting and tending a lot of what I *do* like. I love sweet peas and always mean to dig and manure a trench for them, and make a tall support frame of twigs, at the same time as I am doing that for the runner beans and peas. Once you are embarked upon a job like that, it doesn't really take much more effort to double it up. But July comes and everyone else's sweet peas are a mile high and only then do I remember. So I rely on neighbours with a glut to give me some for the house. Sweet peas, like their edible cousins, will divide and multiply the more they are picked. They do not last very long indoors, but they smell sweet indeed and their sugar-almond pastels are so pretty.

I like to see flowers growing in the way old-fashioned country gardeners always had them, in rows among the vegetables, with the sweet peas up behind the potatoes. Sweet williams grow wonderfully well like this, to be harvested with the carrots and the tiny spring turnips. If I were only allowed one flower in the garden I should be happy with sweet williams, for their spikiness and their clovey scent and their keeping qualities when picked – they will last a month in a vase if you crush the stems and change their water regularly. But sweet williams need to be started from seed in the autumn to flower the following year and I never get around to thinking about flowers in the autumn, so I end up by buying expensive plants in spring, just so as to have them, and with luck they may seed themselves, as wallflowers do, into perennials, albeit rather weakened and straggly.

There are a good many herbaceous border perennials I care for a lot, but whether from lack of nurture or dislike of our soil few will establish themselves and thrive here. A few spread all over, notably french marigolds and forget-me-nots and we have a good number of hollyhocks, pale pink and lemon and white and a deep blood-red. They are in all sorts of odd places and I only wish I could succeed with delphiniums in the same way, for I should love to have a great many of those very tall, very blue soldiers in the flowerbed outside the sitting-room window. They will not stay. Nor will aquilegia, those delicate, winged angels that look as if they are in flight. I have spent many a November hour putting in plants and they have died over the winter. So have ornamental poppies. But I shall try yet again this year, and every year until I succeed. One of the troubles, of course, is that we let the hens out into the garden, although never when there are seedlings about. But nothing can enjoy being so scratched around and loosened. Perhaps I shall give up any efforts to have a decent flowerbed. My heart is not really in it and the flowers know it. I shall go round Barley enjoying and envying other people their colours and scents and begging a few cut flowers where I can.

But there are one or two pipe dreams I have which may come true, if I make a serious effort. I long to see a lot of old roses flourish at Moon Cottage, all sorts of climbers, particularly scented, and to grow some lilies.

I have been warned off old roses by a lot of people. They are prone to every disease, I am told, temperamental and touchy, scarcely worth the trouble. That alone presents me with a challenge, but there is more to the matter than that. Old roses have character, and romance lingering in their pasts. They are like faded old beauties of Victorian and Edwardian country houses. I love their names and their rarity and the way they are ever so slightly blousy, and yet paper-frail, too. They have no resilience, come with no guarantees about their hardiness, or their eagerness to bloom non-stop from June to Christmas, if only you dead-head them. I shall have to restrict myself to varieties which do not mind being exposed, do not have to be pampered with a south-westerly aspect. I doubt if I shall ever be able to achieve the old rose garden I dream of so long as we are at Moon Cottage, but I shall make a start, in the bed near the boundary wall, which will give a little shelter, and perhaps, if things go well, in what is now my unsuccessful herbaceous bed, too. Old roses, alba roses, tea and damask and moss roses, most of them richly scented, many of them white or pink, which I prefer to reds and mauves. Belle de Crécy, Duchesse d'Angoulême, Félicité Parmentier, Madame Hardy, Wife of Bath, Mousseline, Old Pink Moss, all of them will have a place and then, if I can find wall and fence space enough, I shall have the climbers, and three above all.

Albertine, of course. If there were only one rose in the world I should want it to be Albertine, that glorious cascade of the pinkest pink. If I had a very high wall, I should like it tumbling over every inch of it. As it is, I have a small Albertine, growing over part of the low stone wall beyond the apple tree, where it has accommodated itself very happily. Up against the north wall of Moon Cottage, facing the Fen, I have begun to train a Gloire de Dijon, because it will tolerate the aspect. I should have liked to dare the incredibly beautiful Madame Alfred Carrière, and her cousin, Mrs Herbert Stevens, but there is not enough room for them to spread luxuriantly, or enough good rich soil below, in which to root them satisfactorily. If we removed the paving slabs all the way round the inner edge of the house, we could dig in manure and bone-meal and hope to have more climbers, primarily a scented honeysuckle. There is a cottage further up the lane whose whole front beneath its thatch is covered on one side with the rose Albertine and on the other with a sweetly-scented honeysuckle, and the two meet in the middle, to entwine and entangle in each other's arms over the front porch. To walk by on a warm June evening is to be transported.

The kitchen side of Moon Cottage, on the old wall that faces in towards the village, and is a little protected by the fence opposite and Mr Elder's cottage alongside, is covered with a very overgrown wisteria, which I do not greatly care for, and a deep purple, small-flowered clematis, which I do. Getting rid of the wisteria will be a major operation, it is so well-established and rampant in all directions. Some of its foliage creeps and curls right in through the bedroom windows by June each year. There is a family dispute about it, for the others like the thing, but I plan to persuade them that they will like a pink, spring-flowering clematis, or a Mrs Herbert Stevens, even better.

Summer means sunflowers – better called by their exquisitely apposite French name, *tournesol*. It is folly to try and grow them very tall here, of course, the wild winds of the early autumn nights bend and break their thick stems and bow their great shaggy heads to the ground, but I do try nevertheless, because I love them so, their bright faces and open-golden look, and the way the bees swarm about them, I should like a whole marching line of them up against the wall near the woodshed. This year, we sowed two packets of seeds, and only a dozen plants came through. When they had reached what seems to be a vulnerable stage, a height of about six inches, half of these died, yet they are supposed to grow as easily as weeds. I have given them manure and peat, but perhaps they prefer not to be so richly fed. Next year, I shall leave them to seed themselves, and grow where they will.

The heads, when they go to seed, come into the house to be dried and then are hung out on a branch of the apple tree. A lot of birds come to feed off them and, if we are really lucky, there may be a goldfinch or two, a rare treat.

As soon as I have my conservatory, I shall make a serious attempt to grow some lilies, in pots, which is really the only way you *can* give them the exact soil conditions each particular variety likes best, and also the only way to move them about the place, according to the sun and shade. They look lovely in pots, too, though a really fine border thick with lilium candidum or regale is a sight to behold. I prefer those which are either pure white, or flushed through faintly with another colour, or tinged with it just at the heart – like Green Magic. They can be the most perfect flowers, but can also easily tip over that narrowest of dividing lines between splendour and absolute vulgarity. There are some hideous examples in the showier catalogues, violent orange and livid lemon, spotty or crudely streaked – as against delicately freckled.

One of the best things about lilies, of course, is their amazing scent. I shall put my pots of them under open windows, or beside an open door in the cool conservatory or the porch, leading from the front door, and be overpowered.

My mother thought lilies morbid funeral flowers, and could not bear to look at their stiff, waxy whiteness, nor smell what to her was the sweet stench of decay and death. Perhaps I find that hint of Victorian melancholy and funereal pomp in them attractive. If I had my fantasy garden, among the beds and beds of madonna lilies there would be a statue or two, of a winged angel, madly grieving.

Under the shade of the apple tree is an area of old paving stones, pocked and stained and mossy. We have lately had them re-laid, because they were badly sunken and loose here and there, with dangerous cracks and edges. But we did not want to replace them with any new ones, which would have been bald and boringly uniform in tone and size. Nor, of course, did we want that ugliest of uglies, crazy paving. We had toyed with the idea of doing the job ourselves until we each lifted just one slab and nearly broke our backs. Two stalwart young men, calling themselves garden contract engineers, came, and made an excellent job, giving us a new-old area of paving, the stones still slightly askew, still mossy and mellow, but safe and level on a firm cement base. They did not cement between the stones, but instead sand was brushed to and fro until it settled in the crevices and is now ready for us to plant small old-fashioned scented pinks. Country gardens always had at least

a few of these, in cracks, along borders, coming out of spaces between the dry stones on walls, with their clove and pomander
fragrance and muted colours, slightly serrated edges. They are
modest flowers, a far cry from the stiff, artificially bright carnations
of wedding bouquets and floral tributes, and there are several
specialist firms who have kept the many rarer varieties going. But
Lady Grace, in her honeysuckle- and Albertine-covered cottage,
has them too, and has promised me cuttings in the autumn.

The border all around the paving is edged with thyme, which can,
like all herbs, straggle and get out of hand, but can be splendid if
kept well trimmed back, boskily-scented and purple-flowered,and
very useful in the kitchen. I like plants that work twice for their keep.

Until I actually had a fair-sized garden, I believed that you dug in
the autumn, did nothing in the winter, sowed and planted in spring
and gathered in summer, and when you were not tripping about
with a basket, in a floppy straw hat, sat about enjoying the flowers in
the sunshine.

But summer is in some ways the hardest work time of all, and
much of it is done when it's hot or humid or both, which makes it far
harder. What I also did not appreciate is that digging and raking
and heaving things about goes on all through the summer, and let
no one kid you otherwise. There is the earthing up of potatoes
several times, there is the patch you cleared and dug for the planting
of leeks in July which became overgrown again with all manner of
weeds, when it rained over that weekend you went away. There is
compost and manure to lug about for establishing a strawberry bed
in early August. If you are reclaiming land which has never before
been used for vegetables and perhaps has been neglected altogether
for some years, perennial weeds do not die satisfactorily after you
have strolled among them with a hoe for a few evenings, they have to
be chopped down and dug in, until they give up, or else, like
bindweed and ground elder, they have to be rooted up by hand with
bent back.

Once my second garden over in the old orchard had been cleared
and rotavated, it had to be re-dug more finely by hand and then

raked over several times, then weeded again by hand week in week out after everything was planted, throughout the first spring and summer. That garden, though, began to pay for itself within weeks. The soil is so rich and crumbly and productive, everything has cropped easily and in abundance. It has been hard work, and a treasure-trove. The cottage garden is harder work and we get only a fair reward on the heavy clay, and that after the soil has been dug and double dug, manured and composted time and again.

I have now eliminated all the vegetable crops that I did not want to grow, either once or again, and had a try at everything we do want and can grow, and learned a lot, each year, about siting, and the temperament of varieties, so that by limiting myself and specialising a little, I hope to produce, within a few years, really first-class specimens of my chosen produce, in some quantity.

The worst problem during the last glorious summer was drought, and that after one of the wettest springs on record, when the ground was boggy and cold until well into June. Everything was some weeks late in getting started at all, but once the sun did begin to shine, the soil in the Moon Cottage kitchen garden began to harden and harden, and congeal into great brick-like lumps, and, finally, to crack open, though over in the orchard it soaked up the early rain like blotting paper, retained much of it, while drying on top to a nice, soft powder. Perfect.

But, fortunately, the dry spell was twice broken, at the end of July, and three weeks later, by tremendous storms and rain which deluged down for twenty-four hours at a time, nicely soaking everything, though also, alas, beating down some beans and peas, and snapping them off, in spite of their stakes, and giving a long drink to all the dormant weeds.

That second summer in Barley, the kitchen garden at the cottage was planted as follows.

Potatoes

28 lbs of first earlies. I planted them out in mid-April and there was no trouble with frost. The varieties were Irish Peace, Sharpe's Express and Vanessa, the flavour of the first being disappointingly

bland and the yield of Vanessa minimal. I began to lift in early June, when we had several meals of delicious bird's-egg-sized potatoes, steamed in their skins and eaten with melted butter, but because of all the spring rain the tubers swelled quickly and, in terms of weight, there was a bumper yield.

Potatoes lose their subtlety of flavour within a few hours of being pulled up, so this is one crop I plan to have every year in quantity.

Courgettes

I dug in huge quantities of farmyard manure in three areas of the garden, and into this, with only a thin covering of soil, I sowed two packets of courgette seeds. I gave away at least half the resulting plants, and set out the three dozen remaining. These grew to elephantine proportions, with leaves like rhubarb, very spiky stems and masses of flowers each day. From mid-July until the first frosts well into October, I picked an average of fourteen pounds per week, more in the height of their growth, and one or two fruits that were missed in the dense tangle of undergrowth ran to marrows in no time, so we had a double crop. I could have supplied a small shop, or sold them at the gate, if there were any passers-by, but I am more than happy to have a glut of courgettes, and I have collected a lot of good recipes for using them, both as an accompanying vegetable, and as a main course in their own right. They are so easy to grow a child would have no trouble in harvesting well from a few seeds, and it is really not sensible to pay upwards of thirty pence a plant in the garden centre when a packet of seeds costs less and will yield a great number.

Beans

Broad beans and most of the dwarf French beans have been a failure. I sowed three varieties of the latter and, apart from a few plants here and there along a couple of rows, my only real success was in the orchard garden, with a fine crop of dwarf burgundy. In the cottage garden the soil was too wet, too cold, too heavy.

Peas

Six rows were sown, of Kelvedon Wonder and Feltham First and Meteor, and two of an eat-all pea called Sugar Snap (not the true mange-tout). Again, all the early sowings failed to germinate, and the later succeeded only fairly well. The first couple of pickings were reasonably good for half the rows and poor over the remainder. Then, for no discernible reason, the plants began to go pale, shrivel and die. They were kept well watered, fed with liquid manure when the pods were forming and filling, weeded and picked over regularly. Gardening writers say that peas are either a great trial and a trouble to grow, or else, depending, I suppose, on who and where you are, not a bit of bother. Next year I shall change site and varieties, and see what happens. They are a vegetable worth working at, with a delicate flavour and a succulence that cannot be bought or stored. I remember that once my mother grew a few peas a neighbour saved for her. They climbed up a scruffy back garden fence, were not taken a great deal of notice of, and we picked pounds and pounds of pods. Maybe it was the sea air, but I shall keep on trying.

Shallots

Planted out in a very poor, heavy clay area of the garden in wet early March, they nevertheless yielded a reasonable return for almost no work at all, though the bulbs were small. Next time, I shall site them in a richer, lighter area and double the quantities of feed. I pulled them on the first of August, and they lay drying in the blazing sun for two days on some chicken wire, folded up to let the air circulate below. I rubbed off the loose skin, cut the stalks and stored them. They will keep us going for a month or two. We use a lot, chopped up finely in salads, or in place of onions, if I want a mild flavour and small quantity.

Garlic

I tried a row of this near the shallots. It was a total failure. It should have humus-rich, well-fed soil of a crumbly consistency. This was so hard the shoots could scarcely penetrate it at all and the bulbs did not develop. But, again, it is worth persevering, and improving the garlic's growing conditions, because greengrocers who get supplies of really large, juicy garlic are hard to find; so often, you are offered a little plastic net of shrivelled, even mouldy bulbs, with green shoots running through their centres.

Spinach

There are three rows of perpetual spinach (spinach beet) sown in

May and July, and cropping richly. The only work necessary is some weeding by hand, and with a hoe between the rows, and picking. An ideal crop, and one of the cheapest ways to feed a family on vegetables.

Lettuce

Four rows, sown directly into their cropping area, not thinned at all, nor allowed to grow very big and hearty. But this amount was too much for us, so I let one row bolt, and set the tortoise Theodore down the middle of it.

As the potatoes and peas were finished, and the ground dug over again, I planted out a lot of kale, which I grow to feed the chickens during the winter when they have no green shoots to scratch about for. We find it too strong to eat as a vegetable ourselves, but as the chickens turn its vitamins and iron into eggs for us to eat, and manure for the ground, the whole thing is a neat cycle.

I also put out a few leeks, and a dozen strawberry runners left over from the main beds, in the orchard. But the chief winter crop, as usual, in the kitchen garden, is celeriac, a great deal of it, planted out in June, and a little more in August, to keep us going through the winter. It needs weeding carefully, planting shallowly so that the bulb is exposed above the soil, as it grows, and feeding well from late summer on, so that the bulbs swell. But it is an attractive plant, with rich green, decorative foliage, not too tall.

I had intended to sow Florence fennel this year, but there was not enough room, and this needs such good, rich soil to yield decent bulbs (not to mention a lot of sun at the right time, which is why it grows so well in Italy) that I shall only attempt it in the orchard.

Over there, by June, things were looking very good indeed.

Permanent Beds

Globe artichokes (Gros Vert de Laôn). Thirty plants, set out in May. They require very wide spacing, and they grow tall, and have to be protected from frost with straw in autumn or early winter. They form the top right-hand corner of the garden, and we shall begin cutting them next year. They were expensive to buy and they have to be kept well watered when establishing themselves, but what a rare sight they are, with their tall, grey-green spiky foliage and green fruits tinged with purple. Between them, and the asparagus bed, is the long row of runner beans. They climbed very fast, produced hundreds of scarlet flowers, which were alive with bees, and dense foliage – almost too dense. We began picking them during the first week in August, and after that took off several pounds a week until well into October. Apart from the tricky, but quite entertaining, business of erecting their cane support frame eight feet high, they were absolutely no trouble at all, yet they can be temperamental things. I have an uncle in Wales who has always grown the same variety in the same way, and they have done wonders, yet now for some reason he has masses of foliage but no flowers, hence, of course, no beans. My neighbour Albert Baker's beans were an inch or two above the ground when mine had reached the top of their frame and were starting back down the other side. Other people hereabouts have had patchy germination and spindly plants, or few flowers or insufficient pollination by the insects, whereas their next-door neighbours have had record crops.

In August, a storm beat down a lot of the beautiful but delicate asparagus fern, and I had to stake it all. I then fed it with a seaweed-based liquid manure, for asparagus grows naturally on sea margins and, if you can bring back some of the seaweed itself and strew it about the bed in autumn, so much the better for your crop.

The seed bed yielded a good success rate of white- and purple-sprouting broccoli plants, and leeks, both of which I put out in July. They are if anything coming on too well in the rich soil. I don't want them to form too much lush green growth in a mild autumn or they will run to seed, or be too weak to stand the winter cold, but how to hold them back? The other successful seedlings have been the small turnips, Jersey navets, which look like creamy-white carrots, picked very young, while still small. There is also another perpetual spinach bed here, which has been yielding four or five pounds per picking (once every ten to twelve days).

It was in the orchard garden that the French beans did so well, and the mange-touts (Carouby de Maussane) climbed to a height of seven feet rapidly, and yielded very well over a long period. They need shelter and sunshine and very careful training in the early stages.

Our fruit-growing is in its infancy, but it is the growth area of the future here. The world is full of fruit farms, where people go to pick their own produce, and this has meant that fewer and fewer individual gardeners are bothering with fruit at all, for it is a certain amount of trouble, and costs a fortune in netting. But, if you do have the space, consider growing your own fruit, after thinking of all the disadvantages of 'pick your own' farms.

You will have to drive there, perhaps twenty miles or so, which costs money. You will then have to get very tired picking a large quantity of fruit, to make the journey worthwhile. This will then have to be frozen, bottled or made into jams and jellies and pies – more work. And fruit farms are not particularly cheap either. Whereas, once you have invested in the plants, canes and bushes and trees, and they are established, you have the joy of those very precious first strawberries and raspberries, and the continuing crops over a longish period, you can pick just as many as you need at one time, unless you want to spend one glorious afternoon up to your elbows in gooseberries, and be done with it. The fruit farmers only grow large-yielding varieties, and these often lack subtlety of flavour. Concentrating on these en masse means that the older, perhaps more temperamental kinds will gradually die out, and more variety and richness in the world will be lost to standardisation in size, colour and shape.

The only fruit we inherited at Moon Cottage was a straggling old gooseberry bush, all mixed up with a bramble that comes over the wall from the Buttercup field, and a dense patch of vicious nettles. Stripping that bush is indeed a hard and painful labour and we emerge scratched, prickled and stung. But how we appreciate every last little green gooseberry, at the end of it all. There are not very many – about six pounds this year, but the bush is an old one, on a very exposed site, and has been neglected for years.

Last year I bought twenty canes of autumn-fruiting raspberries, called Zeva, and established them at the back of the big herbaceous bed near the house. Not the best spot, but they are said to tolerate some shade, and I wanted to begin with a late variety because it is good to have some of this most delicious of all fruits after the July glut, and because it grows only eighteen inches or so in height and does not need staking. One third of the canes died almost at once, and the rest had a poorish yield in the first year, which was to be expected, but an excellent one thereafter. I shall plant another two rows of them, as well as summer varieties (especially Lloyd George, whose flavour is unmatchable) when I reclaim the next area of Albert Baker's orchard, for fruit.

In our first year at Moon Cottage I planted thirty alpine strawberry plants (a variety called Baron Solemacher) in the shady border opposite the kitchen window, where nothing much else will grow. They look pleasant enough, and from June until the first frosts they have yielded a bowl of tiny, sweetly-flavoured fruits, every day. Jessica has them to herself, for tea or even for breakfast. They would not be worth growing in large quantities, but for this sort of site they are exactly the right thing, and would do well in a vegetable garden border, too.

Our principal strawberry bed was established in the orchard garden on July 29, 1981, after we had watched the Royal Wedding ceremony on television. It was a very hot, humid day, and I had not been able to prepare the ground properly beforehand, so all at once we dug four trenches, and carted three wheelbarrows full of manure and two of compost across the field from the house, and laid them down and forked them in and then planted forty pot-grown strawberry plants, and watered them well with water we carried, also. We finished at about nine o'clock in the evening, after numerous mugs of tea, and glasses of juice, and we ached in every limb and were being eaten alive by midges and gnats that settle in clouds over the orchard from late afternoon on. Our personal contribution to the marriage of the Prince and Princess of Wales was appropriate, I realised, as I soaked in a hot bath that night, because, quite coincidentally, the variety of strawberry is called Royal Sovereign.

Food

S UMMER FOOD means as much as possible from the garden and I
often like to use vegetables not only as an accompaniment to
meat or other main-course items, but in various combina-
tions, as a meal in their own right. This is made easier by having our
constant supply of fresh eggs.

Soufflés have a reputation for being difficult to make, but I have
never found them so, so long as I have an electric hand whisk and
the people are at the table waiting for the soufflé, rather than the
other way around. They can be made out of all sorts of green
vegetables puréed; spinach is delicious, so are courgettes, and the
spears of broccoli or asparagus. The principle is the same for them
all. Steam, or lightly cook in boiling water, the vegetable, put
through a sieve or mouli, and incorporate the purée into the butter
and flour sauce base when it has nicely thickened, before you add
the stiffly-beaten egg whites. Soufflés with these vegetable additions
sometimes take longer to cook than the recipe books claim – unless
you like their centres to be very runny. I always allow ten minutes
more than the stated time.

You don't have to incorporate cheese, or sprinkle it on the top,
but if you do – and the flavour can be a bit bland otherwise – use
Parmesan, freshly grated if possible, from a block kept in the fridge.
I have never served a soufflé to guests, because you need to spend
such time in the kitchen and use up rather a lot of dishes, pans and
cutlery, right at the beginning of the meal, but we eat them
ourselves, often with a salad to follow.

People complain about gluts of home-grown vegetables, and you
can find plenty of articles advising how to freeze, bottle, dry or

otherwise preserve. It depends how much produce you have, how much you mind whether it is fresh or not, and what your general eating habits are, as to whether you want to store mountains of any one variety. We like and eat a lot of vegetables, and prefer them fresh; I do freeze a very little but, when there is a glut, we tend to live on them for the duration, and take the rest to non-gardening friends. I have a small freezer on top of the main refrigerator and mainly use it for freezing things like purées of vegetables, ready-cooked dishes, such as courgette, onion and tomato ragout (a sort of ratatouille without the aubergines and peppers), and portions of casserole of vegetables.

We are particularly fond of soup and eat almost as much of it in summer as in winter – cold. Delicately-coloured, subtly-flavoured and chilled soups, made of fresh vegetables, are a beautiful way to start a meal, with the same simple base of a chicken or vegetable stock or milk and water, and with a thickening of potato purée, or a little cornflour, or the addition of egg yolk. The chosen vegetable is puréed or put through the mouli, and mixed well, preferably in a liquidiser, into the stock, and everything seasoned, before being chilled, and later, sprinkled with chopped tarragon or chervil, chives or parsley. Try cucumber, courgette, watercress, spinach, broad bean (using the pods too) and pea, or chervil only.

When all your tomatoes have ripened at once (and these do not freeze successfully) you can make fresh tomato soup, with basil if you have it – basil goes with tomato as mint with new potatoes; it is a touchy herb, and Stanley, who is the herb expert, now keeps it under glass, in pots, all the year. It can be put outside, but unless the soil is very rich and the site both sunny and sheltered, *and* kept well watered, the basil will fail.

All these summer soups freeze very well and lose precious little of their flavour or texture in the process. I often make a double or triple quantity and freeze some in plastic beakers or ice cube trays.

Eggs and vegetables mean quiches, as well as soufflés, and a savoury quiche, with a good tomato or green salad, is one of our regular supper dishes. I make them using all kinds of green vegetables, with tomatoes, onions, cheese, herbs, eggs and cream or top of the milk. I find pastry-making a bore and, if I had a large enough freezer, I should certainly fill it once every month or so with a lot of flan cases, on the principle that, if I am going to be bored, I may as well be bored in spades, for the whole of an afternoon, and have done.

We like vegetables as starters to a meal, or as a lunch in their own right, with fruit and cheese to follow. I have begun to grow globe artichokes because we all like them so much, and particularly Jessica who, in her eating habits, is a curious mixture of the extremely wary conservatism shown by all small children and bold strokes of adventurousness. When she was two, she watched us going about the curious and fascinating business of eating artichokes, and asked for a leaf. We gave it to her, she pulled it solemnly between her tiny milk teeth and said, 'Mmmmmm, lovely,' and now she will consume a huge one with gusto. She prefers them unadorned, but Stanley makes a delicious vinaigrette which incorporates finely-chopped shallots and parsley.

Apart, obviously, from asparagus in its short season, other good vegetable starters are very young leeks, steamed and served cold with a vinaigrette, or fresh, tiny French beans, cooked until still crunchy, and served either the same way, or with a delicious dressing made of eggs, lemons and oil, heated until thickening, and poured over the vegetable. This can be served hot, or left to go cold.

The one serious glut we have in summer is of courgettes and I use them two or three times a week in various recipes. Apart from a soufflé or a quiche, I have an excellent, though rather rich recipe, for courgettes cooked for about ten or twelve minutes, drained as much as possible – even dried out a little in a pan over a low flame – chopped a bit and spread over a flat fireproof dish. You then mix two eggs with a quarter of a pint of cream and four ounces of grated Gruyère cheese, pour this over the courgettes and cook in a very hot oven for fifteen minutes – i.e. until puffy and golden brown on top. With this, plain, good wholemeal bread and a green salad to follow are all that you require to make a surprisingly filling summer meal.

There is an easy casserole made in a similar way, but the cooked and chopped courgettes are topped with sliced tomatoes, then more courgettes, and so on in layers, and finished off with grated Cheddar cheese, mixed with fresh breadcrumbs then baked for half an hour or so, until the top is crunchy.

Courgettes bake beautifully in the oven alongside chicken joints or lamb chops, and you can also bake them in foil parcels with a bit of butter and salt and black pepper. They can be stuffed with mushrooms (an awful nuisance), battered and quickly deep-fried (rather indigestible) and simply sautéed in butter (luxurious). They are altogether a very versatile vegetable, and a tremendous improvement on the woolly, English giant marrow, into which a courgette will grow if you leave it for a few days too long on the plant. Which is why, if you go on holiday in August, you need a friendly neighbour with a taste for courgettes to come in and pick the plants over every couple of days.

Spinach has had a bad reputation in the past, and it is easy to understand why people are revolted by that dark green, over-cooked substance resembling pond slime that used to be served by cooks trained to boil every vegetable to within an inch of its life, and is still what you get if you buy it chopped and ready-frozen. The combination of this with lukewarm, runny eggs dumped on top of it has repelled many a poor child (or adult) put on to an iron-rich diet. But if it is freshly picked, when still young, and eaten either raw, in a variety of salads, or very lightly cooked, this is one of the most succulent of all vegetables. It really does suffer from being more than half an hour off the plant, but even if you do not have a garden, you could grow a row of perpetual spinach on a terrace, in a windowbox, in a growing-bag laid along a balcony.

If it is picked when very small, you need only peel off the central stalk, but the moment the leaves are getting large, all the stalky, stringy veins have to be stripped which is a long, tedious job, particularly because, as spinach shrinks in the pan, you need huge quantities per person.

When this deadly dull job is done, put the leaves into a giant saucepan with only the water left clinging to them after you have washed them thoroughly, or else into a steamer, cook gently for far less time than you might suppose, and certainly no more than ten minutes, with the lid off, and push the vegetable about a bit with a wooden spoon to prevent sticking. Take it out when tender, press any water out in a colander with the back of another, thick wooden spoon – there will be a lot. I have a friend who reserves this in a jug and drinks it when it is cold. Full of vitamins, minerals and other nutrients essential to healthy life and growth, but I couldn't face it myself.

Next, drop the wet mass of spinach, splat, on to a chopping board and cut it about with a very sharp knife. Never purée it unless you are making soup or soufflé, or you will have the pond-slime I spoke of. You can leave the spinach now and re-heat it whenever you like. Then, you just add as much or as little butter as you like and season with plenty of salt and black pepper, warm through thoroughly but gently, again moving it about constantly with a spoon, to prevent sticking and burning. Your spinach should now have texture and firmness, be a bit buttery but not too much and with a delicious, earthy flavour. It will go well with chicken, calves' liver, gammon, or salmon trout, form the basis of an Egg Florentine dish, or be extremely nice eaten all by itself.

We like spinach raw, in a salad with watercress, or in a bacon and spinach combination.

Crisply fry some streaky bacon and crumble. Mix with raw, young leaves of spinach, carefully washed. Dress either with a good vinaigrette, made on the oily side with the very best olive oil you can find, *or*, pour the hot fat from the bacon pan over the salad, mix quickly and serve at once.

Some olive oil is disgusting, but we still have golden memories of one that came from paradise. For a wedding present, a French friend brought us a pestle and mortar, carved out of olive wood from his own trees, and a litre whisky bottle full of his own olive oil. It was a deep greenish gold colour, had the consistency of motor-oil and such a flavour as we have never encountered anywhere again.

One day in June, I came back from London on the train, and when you do that you get an excellent view not only of what people grow on their allotments and in their back gardens, in all the suburbs of the cities, the small towns and villages, but you also see how much shrubbery there is, wild shrubbery, along embankments and cuttings and snickets, around the edges of playing fields and waste ground and factory yards and office forecourts, and car parks, how many hedges and ditches, as well as more cultivated belts of shrubbery at the bottom of gardens. And, in June, all these green margins are starred with the great, flat creamy flowers of the elder tree. I had no idea how densely populated Southern England was with it and of course it only reveals itself so obviously in the spring, when it is in blossom, and September, when it fruits – though these are less easy to spot from any distance.

I collected my car from the station and drove home to Barley and noticed the elders again, through the town and up all the country lanes, until I reached the last one, against the far wall of our own garden, near the woodshed. And, of all the hedgerow foods which we prize, elderberries come second only to blackberries and crab apples, and, for subtlety and delicacy of flavour, elderflowers crown all. They last for about three weeks. One day, when they were at their finest, I met Primrose in the lane carrying a basket piled high with them. She makes enough elderflower wine to keep them in everyday drink the whole year, and some elderflower champagne for special occasions. I am not a wine-maker, and never intend to be, so I left her to it and hope I can swop a few jars of this or pounds of that, later in the year, for one of her precious bottles, though Primrose makes and grows everything, including honey, so I doubt if I shall be able to fill any gap in her store-cupboard.

Elderflowers have the flavour of Muscat grapes and that is indescribable. With only a few of them, Stanley makes the best of all water-ices; he has experimented with all sorts of fruits and other flavours for sorbets, but I like elderflower the most, and it is very simple.

You need:
6 oz sugar
1 pint water
1 egg white
Juice of 2 and rind of 3 lemons
4 elderflower heads

Combine everything except the egg white and lemon juice. Stir over a low heat until the sugar dissolves. Boil for ten minutes. Cool. Add lemon juice. Strain carefully. Freeze until mushy (about an hour). Beat with a fork or hand-whisk. Stiffly beat the egg white and fold it in. Freeze again for another hour. Stir. Leave in the freezer until needed. If very solid, let it thaw just slightly in the fridge before bringing to the table. You can garnish the centre with a head of elderflowers, pressing it down slightly and freezing for the last hour only.

Gooseberries are the first of the summer fruits and they coincide with the elderflowers, in Moon Cottage garden, if we're lucky. The two combine perfectly, in a jam, or a jelly. (You tie the elderflower heads in a little bag of muslin and steep them in the hot jelly while it is still boiling, by tying it to the handle of the preserving pan with string and suspending it over the side.)

Strawberries and raspberries are best eaten in huge quantities during their seasons, with sugar and Jersey cream. But there is also, of course, the inestimable Summer Pudding, combining raspberries with red and black currants inside a bread mould, until the juices soak through completely. With luck, you can have this ambrosial dish three weekends running in a summer.

We are not great dinner party-givers. Having to go to them, unless I know everyone and then they turn into a party for old friends, depresses me utterly and, with a job each and a small child, our lives do not sort with formal entertaining. Usually we have whole families to Sunday lunch, winter or summer, sometimes with the adults eating on the round table in the dining room, and the children just next door at the kitchen table, an arrangement that suits all parties, and, as there are always plenty of willing hands with the washing-up, it doesn't seem to matter about the double amount of clearing.

But just occasionally, perhaps twice a year, we do have four friends to supper, carefully chosen, to go well together, and often, indeed, knowing one another already, though we don't always realise that until everyone arrives. We had one such party early in July, and to celebrate something or other, drank a bottle of champagne at the beginning of the evening, sitting outside in the last of the sunshine, talking and watching the black cat Polly rush to the very topmost branch of the apple tree and then walk delicately, just as far as was prudent, along to the end of one branch, before peering down at us, a head and two huge yellow-green eyes through the leaves, like the Cheshire cat.

Then we went inside. We ate artichokes and a salmon trout. With this there were mange-touts, tiny broad beans, spinach and new potatoes, all from the garden, and a salad of paper thin slices of cucumber dressed in a vinaigrette, and sprinkled with the chopped leaves of fennel. Stanley also made a hollandaise, over which he is prepared to take endless trouble, and after that came one of his masterly green salads. I, who am always pudding cook, had made a big gooseberry tart, the French way, with a custard base of egg yolks and thick cream, on top of which went the fruit, in circles, which is easier to do with gooseberries but requires the skills of a master pâtissière to do with sliced apples. And with that we drank some of the wine called Muscat de Beaumes de Venise which has the flavour of elderflowers – a few heads of which I had steeped in the poaching syrup for the gooseberries.

Then, it was dark. We went back into the garden and sat with our glasses full of the last of that beautiful wine, under the magic apple tree, talking, laughing, and then for a moment, all suddenly silent, as the moon rose and shone on all the fields, near and far, and from Lyke Wood, far below, we heard the owls cry, and the fox cubs yelp, and above our heads, a slight, warm breeze rustled the leaves of the apple tree like silk. It was the happiest of evenings.

Creatures

BY EARLY summer, the six White Leghorn hens were laying well, often an egg each per day, and I was feeling rather pleased with myself. Hens are little trouble. Whoever is first up in the morning fills their drinker with fresh water and their feeder with layers' mash, and lets them out into the hen-run. After lunch when, on the whole, all the eggs for that day have been laid, they are given the run of the whole garden, unless there are any new seedlings, which they make for and scratch up in seconds. At some point in the day I collect the eggs from the nest boxes, and turn over the straw litter to keep it fresh, and in the evening the birds are brought back into the run when I throw a couple of handfuls of corn there. Unlike children, they put themselves to bed at dusk, and all we have to do is drop down their pop-hole, to keep out any foxes and rats.

Things, in early June, were moving along easily in this routine, when the hen Sarah ruptured herself while laying an egg. She trailed about the run for a couple of days looking unhappy and messy. I sought advice. But hens are not good survivors, they lose what will they have to live very quickly, and on the third morning Sarah separated herself from the others, didn't eat or drink, and tucked herself in a quiet corner of the henhouse on a straw bed. At lunch-time, I fetched Violet, who wrang her neck for me. I should be able to do it myself, yes, and I shall have to learn, but I would rather cull someone else's birds than my own. Many hen keepers, I know, feel exactly the same.

Then there were five. Until Rosie went broody. Nonsense, they said, modern egg-laying birds never go broody, they've had the instinct bred out of them. By August, three out of the five had been broody. Nature will out. Often, the broodiness doesn't last more than a few days, but Rosie had been sitting, tight as a limpet, on every egg that was laid, for a week, so Violet borrowed her, set her on eleven assorted Maran and bantam eggs, and waited to see what would happen, though without much confidence. Three weeks later, all the chicks hatched out and Rosie proved an excellent mother. Jessica and I walked up the lane to visit the tiny, cheeping yellow fluffballs periodically, and each time we went, they had grown so fast and changed so much we did not recognise them, and in the end they were gangling adolescents, all legs and newly-sprouted feathers, like boys' first beards, and Rosie was sent home, her mothering done.

At the same time, I arranged to have some more hens, four Rhode Island Reds on point of lay, and collected them that same day. Breeders say you cannot introduce new hens among old, that war will break out, and the hens tear each other apart, that the established ones will hog all the food and water, while the new-comers sit and stare. For a week, there was some hostility, but the brown hens were confident and quite large and soon fitted into the pecking order. It was poor old Rosie who suffered the most, back in her old home; among the original companions she was utterly rejected, chased round the run, pecked at, kept away from the food and water troughs, so that in desperation I took to letting all the rest out into the garden, and keeping Rosie in, to feed separately and peacefully. Her salvation was her decision to join forces with the brown newcomers and now, although peace and harmony reign in the henhouse, she will roost among them rather than with the other Leghorns.

The Rhode Islands began to lay after a fortnight, big, brown eggs, in quantity, and I took on more customers. If we had the space, I should keep perhaps four dozen hens, including some pure breeds like the Marans, silky bantams and a dozen or so plain, brown hens to provide us with a reliable egg supply.

Hens are not the most intelligent creatures in the world, but neither are they as stupid as, say, sheep, and they do have some rather endearing habits and very different temperaments. Our White Leghorns are inclined to be shy, flighty, even neurotic, but the brown are bold, inquisitive, and friendly, and come into the house, if they get the chance, and always follow me about when I am in the garden. They actually rather like to be picked up and stroked, and they also like delivering me a sharp peck on the ankle, if they are in the mood.

I should like to rear chicks, but have neither space, facilities, nor time, and with a small child, I would never keep a cockerel, for they can be very vicious indeed, and quite without warning. Besides, we have enough of being woken up at dawn – by the magpies.

I loathe magpies, though they are spectacular birds, on the ground and in flight, trailing their long tails. Their habits are hideous, yet they do not have any of the character, and the fascination, of the real hawks, or of owls. They are messy, and they are noisy. A colony of them nests regularly on the fringes of the buttercup field, and from mid-spring into late summer, the parents, and their offspring, would alight on the fence below our bedroom window, any time between five and six o'clock in the morning, there to chatter and screech until, thoroughly roused in every sense, we went to bang loudly on the window. My fingers have never itched for a shotgun until this.

When we had only the white hens, the magpies would land among them, two or three at a time, and attack their feeding trough, and pick up all the spare corn, while the Leghorns cowered together, twittering anxiously, behind the henhouse. When the brown hens arrived, they rushed at the magpies in a mob, flapping their wings and squawking, and they have never set foot in the hen-run since.

If magpies are welcomed neither by us nor by the hens, the green woodpeckers are positively courted, because they are so spectacular and unusual. The village is full of them; round the corner of a lane or walk across the field to the orchard garden, past the three syca-mores, and a yellow, green and red bird will rise up in alarm, making its yaffle-yaffle laugh, and going away in swooping, up and down flight, across to the woods. It was a young one that I first saw at Moon Cottage, on the flat roof outside the study window where I was working. I looked up, to see an extraordinarily ungainly fledgling, grey, all neck and legs and beak, apparently stranded. Its pale eyes stared in alarm, but eventually it went, very uncertainly, into the branches of the apple tree. It had a familiar shape but without the distinctive colouring of the adult's feathers. I could not place it. Then, that afternoon, I glanced out of the window and saw a pair, male and female with the young beside them, excavating an ants' nest beside an upturned stone. They come regularly if they know I have been digging or moving any of the stones, so that ants are exposed, and in late summer, they flock into the apple and the rowan trees of Moon Cottage garden and next door, in the garden of the derelict cottage, where there are a good many old fruit and berry trees. But they are very shy, and if startled will not return the same day.

In that wilderness garden next door we have once or twice seen a great spotted woodpecker, black and white and red, on the ground, and on the trunk of an old tree, and once, just once, he came on to the fence opposite our kitchen window. I thought he might discover the bird pudding in the hanging coconut shell, but he had hardly alighted when he was gone again.

The sparrows fledge family after noisy family in the wisteria that clambers up our west wall, the wrens hatched their brood in the woodshed, but on the whole, in the summer, the garden like all gardens is short of birds. They are hidden away in the trees, or the woods, or else forage for food on the remoter areas of the Fen.

But, in Lyke Wood, the young owls have been reared. We sit quietly outside under the apple tree on warm August nights, when it is dark around nine o'clock. Then, up rises the great pumpkin of a harvest moon, and the fields are still, still, and we wait. And, after a while, the owls begin to cry, the young ones still raucous, their voices unbroken, screeching to their parents, and flying occasionally between the willow trees at the bottom of the Buttercup field, or else up, nearer and nearer, until they may, if we are lucky, come into the wilderness garden, or even to the magic apple tree itself.

I have been fascinated by owls since my childhood. There is something about their shape and their fierce beauty, their mysteriousness and their terrible ways, that I love. Best of all are barn owls, glimpsed, sometimes, in the headlights of the car as we come home, hooded heads like ghosts, like nuns' cowls, and pale, pale feathers, huge eyes. But it is the tawny owls we have here and who emerge from Lyke Wood around dusk, to skim silently over the fields, or to stand still as stones, on fence or post, staring down, biding their times, hoo-hooing softly.

In the late afternoons and early evenings of the summer, go down the lane, stand on the stile, look over towards the wood, and the Fen beyond, and you are almost sure to see flycatchers, on the fencing-posts, for there are clouds of insects to feed on and they dart out and back, out and back a hundred times, small, nervous, delicate birds.

In the field that abuts on the orchard garden, at the top end, nearest the hedge, there are thistles and, in early August, they seed themselves and are covered in their ghostly puff-balls, that fly about in the air and cling to hair and clothing, and on these seed-heads feed goldfinches, masses of them together. When I go through the gap into the garden they rise up like insects and fly in panic to the far side of the field where there are more thistles, flashing gold and scarlet and white.

And suddenly, one hot, drowsy afternoon, we were sitting beside the little pond looking into the water at the lilies, and the tiny fish below, when, all around our heads, we heard a high violin-squeaking and, looking up, saw a party of long-tailed tits, on the move from the wilderness garden into the apple tree and off again, to the rowan, and away in seconds, before we had time to take them in properly.

On the third of August, the sky was gathering for a thunderstorm, the air misty, heavy, still, you could scarcely breathe. I walked up through the village to post a letter and, as I looked up into the sky, saw one swift, circling and swooping, not very high, and rather anxiously. Above the church tower were others, making a lot of noise. This, I said to myself, is the last time I shall see swifts this year, and sure enough, after the next day of torrential rain and mighty storms, when the skies cleared to brightest blue again, they had gone, every one, and in the midst of the blazing sunshine I felt the shadow of the end of summer, the turning of the year.

If you leave Barley by the ridge, after crossing the field footpath that runs along the top you begin to drop gently down again between hedgerows, towards woodland and meadow, and running along, and appearing here and there, before going underground or between the trees, is a broad, shallow stream. I had gone for an afternoon walk with the dog Tinker, and paused, on one of these inclines, to sit down in the sun. It was very hot, very still. I closed my eyes, and the dog lay beside me in the grass. I was reminded of times I spent in a remote part of Dorset, living in a farm cottage, some distance away from any other houses, writing, reading, walking, solitary, as now. But, in spite of the similarity of the countryside, I would never have expected to see here what I often saw then – roe deer. I know they are in the area, there are warning signs on one or two of the roads a few miles away, but it is a fairly busy area, worked by farmers, more thickly populated than those places where deer are most easily and frequently seen, and those that do live in the woodlands around are likely to stay hidden.

One moment, the slope of the field down to the stream and the wood behind were empty, silent, in the heavy afternoon sun. When I looked again, a pair of deer and two fawns had emerged from among the trees and were first drinking from the stream, then grazing. I put my hand on the dog's collar. I doubt if he would have gone after the deer but I did not want any movement or sound, and he might well have barked. Then, after ten minutes or so, the young deer began to play, to chase each other round and round, to skip delightfully, while their parents looked on. They may be pests to the farmers, eating and trampling down the corn crops, and attacking saplings, but deer are the most graceful, pretty creatures and the countryside would be the poorer without them.

What was particularly unusual, though, was for them to be out in the afternoon. Usually, they feed at dawn and dusk, keeping in the shade and ruminating during the daytime. Perhaps the heat made them need water and, once out and in a peaceful spot, the young could not restrain themselves from playing in the sunshine.

After a while, a distant gunshot alarmed them and they vanished into the woodland. We waited, but they did not reappear and the dog and I made for home across the ridge. There was no sound of bird, no sign of any man or beast. I have never seen a deer in these parts again.

Polly the young cat brings a field mouse or a shrew into the house almost every evening, and, sometimes, she has clearly found a nest and gone to pick out the young one by one. She does not injure one but, in the worst way of all cats, carries them loosely in her mouth, sets them down, and then, when they run away, pounces on them again and so on and on, with the poor little mouse squeaking piteously, and scurrying under fridge or dresser, where it stays, and the cat sits, waiting, waiting. We have rescued dozens, though sometimes they simply die of fright, their beautiful, soft bodies stiff and their eyes starting from their tiny heads. When the farmers begin to cut the corn, millions of mouse nests must be disturbed or destroyed. We release a few over the wall into the Buttercup field, but the shrews nest in the garden itself, where they do extremely useful work, keeping down pests.

Late one afternoon, I saw Polly sitting close up to the fence that divides us from Mr Elder's garden. She was absolutely motionless, staring at something, and she continued to sit like that for the next two hours. In the end, I went to investigate, and found some tunnelling beneath one of the fencing posts, and a lot of fine, flung soil. Clearly, a mole had been on its way to us, from Mr Elder's garden, where there are dozens, and Polly had spied it and stopped its progress. I was glad of that. Moles are charming characters, small and pretty; there are at least two beautiful poems about them, one by Andrew Young, and the other by John Clare which, like so much written by that sad, gentle man, is full of pity and regret:

O I never call to mind
Those pleasant names of places but I leave a sigh behind
While I see the little mouldiwarps hang sweeing to the wind
On the only aged willow that in all the field remains,
And nature hides her face while they're sweeing in their chains
And in a silent murmuring, complains.

Moles have always been trapped and shot because, poor, blind, solitary creatures, they are indeed a menace, to gardeners and farmers, and groundsmen; they not only leave their earthy hills all over the place, having excavated as much as ten pounds of soil in a quarter of an hour or so, but they destroy all the earthworms, and earthworms are the gardener's friends. Mr Elder traps moles, other people in Barley have little terriers, which catch them most efficiently. For some reason, although they are only next door, and in such numbers, too, they have not, until this summer, crossed over to us, although I manure the garden heavily, which gives rise to earthworms all right. I don't want a plague of moles, but nor do I want to trap them, so if the cat can simply deter them from making the crossing on to our land, I shall be obliged.

On the last Sunday in August, at about eleven o'clock in the morning, I carried a pile of bolted lettuces and old pea haulms down to the compost heap, and, as I was stuffing it down, I glanced up into the Buttercup field. It was a fine morning, the early mist was rolling back across the Fen and cows and trees and fences were emerging from it in the sunshine. Near at hand, the grass was glittering with dew. And not ten yards away from me, looking straight into my face, was a dog fox, big and bold and handsome, sniffing the air. I waited. He waited. He had been on his way to our garden, there was no doubt, at all, he would have been up and over the stone wall and among the hens in seconds. And the hens were all out of their run and scratching about the garden.

Then the fox caught my scent and turned and went streaking away down the slope towards the willows and up the Rise on the opposite side, brush up, ears pricked, and I called the hens in with a handful of corn, and shut the gate on them, just in case.

Village Life

SUMMER IS a busy time in Barley. In summer, at the end of the village school year, there are the Infant and Junior Sports Days, and the Swimming Gala – for there is a small, above-ground pool, built after much hard fund-raising a few years ago. There is a school carnival every alternate year, and a Playgroup Open Day, and summer outings for everyone.

The Women's Institute has its last formal meeting of the year in June – not that any of our meetings are run in the grand, official manner. After that, in July, with luck there is a social evening in one of the members' gardens, with coffee and home-made cakes and other delicacies, and much admiring of herbaceous borders and fruit bushes, until dark, and the promising of cuttings in autumn, and shared complaints about the wet spring and the absence of pollinating bees. I don't think there is a member of the Barley W.I. who is not a gardener, on large or small scale, and everyone has their own speciality, and their private hints and tips, so that you learn a good deal from simply standing about, eavesdropping.

In August, a lot of people are on holiday, but those who are at home and fit and mobile go on a ramble, usually across the Fen but sometimes up past High Holt and on to the Ridge, then down into one of the neighbouring villages. We set off at six and get home just before dark, and it is all very jolly and haphazard, with plenty of rests, to get the breath and admire the scenery.

In summer in Barley, as in all the villages around, there are cricket matches, on the playing field at the top of the steep hill called Norman Way, where spectators and visiting batsmen waiting to go in and batsmen who have just got out spend as much time looking out across the Fen to the hills beyond, or lying on their backs watching the clouds drift by as they do watching the progress of the match. In the wooden pavilion, the identical model of every other village cricket pavilion up and down the country, the ladies toil over making sandwiches and the place smells of that white dubbin that goes on the boots, of urn tea and freshly-cut cucumber and leather, and on the perimeter of the field, among the tatter of hawthorn and elder bushes, the children play in and out, and during tea the small boys have their own few overs on the pitch itself.

These are the sights and sounds and smells of every English village with a cricket team in summer, they are unchanged since my childhood, when I went, Sunday after Sunday, with my grandfather, to watch matches in half the villages of Yorkshire, if I close my eyes I believe I am still there, hearing the crack of the bat and the spattering applause, and the sudden cry of appeal like a harsh bird call. We have had, at the end of the season, some idyllic afternoons, hot and still, and the shadows have lengthened on the grass so gracefully, during the last overs, the trees around the field have stood so absolutely still, like cut-out trees, dark as dark, with the sun behind them. We have seemed to be in some sort of innocent paradise, where there is no jangling or dissent, no racket and riot from the world, where everything is sorted in friendship and good humour and peace.

Other villages have summer celebrations in plenty. Hope has a Medieval Fair, with everyone in costume and the streets flowing with mead. Quelton has a bi-annual gymkhana and, because the wind often blows from that direction, we hear through the afternoon disembodied voices carrying the names of all the Fionas and Henriettas and Carolines and their winning ponies up the fields towards us.

Worminglee has a Flower Festival, Lyke a Steam Fair, and the Fen Young Farmers stage ploughing and driving contests. There are sheepdog trials and clay pigeon shoots, game fairs and best of all, that wonderful institution, the Flower and Produce Show.

There was once a Horticultural Society in Barley, but it lapsed and no one has seemed anxious to revive it, not because of the amount of work or the cost involved, but because it caused such a lot of bad feeling. It may be a joke to the outside world, trivial matter and all childishness, for people to fall out over the relative merits of flowers and fruit and vegetables. But in a very small community, where everyone lives cheek by jowl, and there are some very strong, very contrary personalities, there will inevitably be local matters, involving opinion and competition, which create animosity.

So, we had to go to Little Lyke one Saturday afternoon in early August to enjoy a Flower and Produce Show in all its glory and rivalry.

It was held in a marquee in one of the fields behind St Leonard's Church, and by half past two the school playground, which had been made over for a car park, was full and the overflow running down the lane behind the Carpenter's Arms. The marquee smelled of hot flowers and tomatoes, and there was a dais, on which stood a table and on *that* were the cups and trophies and shields. Little Lyke has had a Show since 1887, when prizes were freely bestowed by the neighbourhood gentry, and he who wins the Sweet Pea Challenge Trophy keeps, for a year, an elaborate silver object engraved with columns of local names, its magnificence and size far outdoing the present modest scale of the show and the relatively small number of entrants. The names spoke volumes about individual rivalries. J. P. Greet and A. Honeyman had been locked in combat over dahlias for thirty years, the contest swinging now this way for six or seven years, now that for a decade. I speculated about what A. Honeyman had discovered to help him bring on his prize specimens, causing him to win the trophy in an unbroken eleven years, from 1921 to 1932, before J. P. Greet wrested it back again – or what dark deed J. P. Greet had done at dead of night on A. Honeyman's territory, unable to bear the other man's supremacy and his own defeat a moment longer.

The flowers were of the sort I could never grow, even if I desired to, vast and waxen, globular chrysanthemums, stiffly-spiked, peach-coloured gladioli, sunburst dahlias, all grown under intensive conditions, in frames and hothouses and special beds, by single-minded, dedicated men (for this sort of gardening is a masculine activity).

I daresay at much larger shows, especially in the North of England, vegetables are still grown for size, and there are leeks as thick as a man's forearm and marrows the size of meteorites. But, at Little Lyke, everything, though smaller and neater, was of superb quality and looked handsome, having, in all probability, a far better flavour than those colossi. Showmen used to put a special glucose drip to their marrows, and on this diet of sugar and water, and rooted in neat manure, a marrow will take over the world. There were none of these at Little Lyke, and there *were* some vegetables they'd never have stood for in the village shows of my Yorkshire childhood, golden-yellow courgettes and purple-edged French lettuce and the greenish white bulbs of Florence fennel.

There were more women entrants than ever used to be the case then, too. Ladies traditionally entered jams and jellies, chutneys and marmalades and a flower-arrangement, together, possibly, with a plate of three best eggs. But, apart from the champion chrysanthemum and dahlia men, it is the women who do the gardening in many a cottage and house in these villages to-day.

It grew much too hot too soon in the marquee, so we came out and queued for our cups of tea and slices of chocolate cake at the Women's Institute stand, and took them over to the shelter of the churchyard trees which fringed the outer edges of the field. Then a band began to play, a brass band from a big village ten miles away, and after a time the judging began, and we went back inside to see the pink, white and blue cards indicating prize-winners, propped up against the exhibits, and to learn that A. Honeyman (grandson of *the* Honeyman) had carried off the dahlia trophy, yet again.

It was a good summer. Everyone had sunshine and blue skies for their celebrations and the crowds rolled up and the money rolled in, in aid of church towers and bells and roofs, village halls and sports clubs and local charities for the very old and the very young. But the best day of all, the day we had been working towards for a whole year, was in Barley. We didn't have a fête or a carnival or a show or a fair, in Church meadow or on the green or the school playing field. We had all of it rolled into one, called an Open Weekend, involving the entire village. Up and down the lanes, on telegraph poles and gate posts, and boards propped up in the verges, the posters said, 'Barley En Fête', and we were, we were. People opened their gardens and showed them off, and sold plants and flowers, eggs and vegetables, jams and jellies and cakes, on trestle-tables down the streets, there were teas in the W.I. hall and in the Manor House and The Grange; there were tours of Mr Plum's farm and a guided walk down the footpaths to Lyke Wood and across the Fen, and back up the lane on the other side. Lady Grace brought out her pony and trap and gave rides through the village, and it was a joy to see stately old men and fat ladies and city children sitting up there looking pleased. There were pony rides in one field and donkey rides in another, there was a display of flowers in the church, and children's painting and models, in the school, and a magic lantern show by old Canon Days, of Victorian and Edwardian country life. Morris Men came from Dill and Hope, and danced in front of the pub every hour on the hour for two afternoons, and the school recorder band and the junior choir gave concerts, two in the church and one on the green. Every cottage was decorated with flowers and ribbons and bunting, everyone had something to sell or a try-your-luck-stall at the front gate. In Church meadow there was bowling for a pig, and on the Saturday night an ox was roasted and a bonfire lit and everyone went to dance in a marquee on the cricket field.

And people came, from neighbouring villages and the city and from everywhere else under the sun, it seemed, drawn by our posters and the fine weather, off the roads to the north and to London. A good many found Mrs Appleby's long lawn, which she had sprinkled with borrowed deckchairs, and simply sat all afternoon in the sunshine, or the shade of her beech and walnut trees, enjoying the view of the Fen. Lavender's children took parties of six at a time to see their bantam chicks and enterprising Eleanor Field found homes for five of her labrador-cross-unknown mongrel puppies in a single afternoon. There was a demonstration of shoeing by the farrier and of sheep-shearing by Paul Plum and a wheelwright was borrowed from Lockley to make wheels on the corner of Fen Lane, by the pond. In Colonel Cripps's driveway a traditional red and yellow gypsy caravan was open to inspection and so were the old cider presses in his high barn. The cubs and brownies and church choirboys went round collecting litter in huge plastic sacks, and at the end of Sunday it all went on to another bonfire, our beacon for miles around. It was the hottest, happiest, most exhausting of weekends. We lost count of the number of people who came, but not of the money, which was nearly £1,900, towards the restoration and re-hanging of the Barley Bells, and the mending of one of the chancel pillars, which is badly crumbling, and an outing or the Over Sixties, to the seaside.

And now, when I say I live in a village called Barley, they say yes, yes, *we* came to Barley on your Open Day, and it was such fun and everyone was so friendly, and what a wonderful way to celebrate the summer! And so it was.

Then, all at once, the whole village seemed to have gone away on holiday, and the few of us who were left each had a row of keys hanging up and were feeding cats and chickens and goldfish, picking courgettes and runner beans and peas, collecting eggs, checking doors and windows and letter boxes daily. At night, I walked up the lane with Tinker, and there was the harvest moon, lighting my way, and a thicket of stars, but no lights from cottage windows, and no sound anywhere, except the secret ones of night creatures in the hedges and ditches and the pat of the dog's paws. Honeysuckle and late roses smelled sweet from doorways and porches, and the moon had fallen upside down into the pond. I stirred the dark water with my finger and it shattered into silver pieces.

On the corner of the lane, Charley Sleeply sat, still as a stone cat on the top of the wall, but his eyes were on the dog, and when the dog caught sight of him, he vanished.

Pit-pat, pit-pat past the pillar box and down the hill towards the pub, where there were lights and cars and laughter and the knock of skittles, the thud of darts into the cork board, and away again, past more empty houses, with windows reflecting back the moon. And up on to the ridge. A lot of the corn has been cut now, and gathered in, and a combine which caught fire sits in the middle of a half-harvested field like a great, dead dinosaur. Soon, the stubble will be fired, and lines of smouldering red will creep across the fields like slow-burning indoor fireworks, soon they will be ploughed again and the land that was pale, corn-gold will be earthy brown and ridged, smaller-seeming. Soon, the trees will begin to turn.

Down Fen Lane, the moonlight shows up the bramble berries, pale green, but fully formed, and the elderberries, too, and there are nuts on the chestnut trees and bunches of keys on the sycamore and the ash, and acorns on the oak. The plovers have started to flock again, and the swifts have long gone, and the cuckoo, too. We are approaching the year's turning. I can see autumn just ahead and yet, in the middle of the day, when the early mist has cleared, it is still high, high summer. The village is in the doldrums. There are only sixteen of us in church on Sunday, there is no choir, and the decorators have moved into the empty school.

During the last week of August, we go away ourselves, leaving our key, and our animals and our garden, in safe keeping, and for two weeks Barley and the fields and the Fen, the chickens, the vegetables, the plans for this and that, seem very far away. We soak up the sunshine and olive oil and wine and atmosphere of another country.

When we return, the apples have ripened red and the peas are finished, and one of the hens looks as if she has started to moult.

Everybody is home and looking sunburnt, notices begin to appear on the village board, about the beginning of this and the first meeting of that. On Tuesday morning, the school bus rounds the corner of the lane on the stroke of half past eight by St Nicholas clock.

The summer is over.

F OR SOME weeks, everything looks the same, it might still be summer. The leaves on the apple tree are thick and dark and green, the fields beyond are grassy, though there are no flowers at all. Look farther then. The corn has all been cut, and some of the stubble fired, so that those fields are faded yellow and blackened brown, in strips, and one by one they are ploughed, so that the brown earth is visible again. But the trees are, for the moment, as they have been since early July, dusty and dry, but green, still.

The sun still shines in the middle of the day, too, it is a golden September. At noon, it is very hot indeed, we are still wearing cotton clothes, and the children have gone back to school in summer dresses.

But day by day there are slight changes, subtle alterations in shape, in the mood of the season, it is as though everything is slipping and sliding very gradually downhill, like some great high hayrick sinking softly into itself as it dries. The year has turned and it is autumn, though we do not fully acknowledge it.

Fruits have been visible on the apple tree and on all the various trees around me, for some time, and now they are reddening, ripening and swelling and darkening. Stand at the top of the stone steps, now, looking through the branches and they are what you first notice. Turn your head. In the wilderness garden of the derelict cottage, the apple trees are bending with fruit, berry-red and huge. Our apples are tiny and hard, sour, more or less inedible, even after cooking. This is an old tree, after all. We do not keep it for what we can get from it – or, at least, not in terms of fruit.

There is a mist every morning now and until eight o'clock or nine it is quite cold, go outside and stand for a few minutes under the apple tree and you will shiver. There are wasps crawling and droning about all over the fallen fruit at my feet. There is a dew on the grass so thick that it seems to have rained heavily in the night. Across the bramble bush that has grown up from the field on the other side of the low stone wall and begun to scramble over it, cobwebs are strung about, delicate, tingling with tiny tiny drops of moisture, silver as mercury beads.

Then, I do not go outside in the early morning for several days, because I have a head cold, and there is rain, and when next I do, the leaves of the apple tree have begun to yellow and fade, that is quite clear to see, and looking down the field towards the line of willows, I see that they, too, are slightly paler, and so it goes on, though it will be some weeks yet before the whole valley of trees has turned and begun to fall.

There is a smell in the air, the smell of autumn, a yeasty, damp, fruity smell, carrying a hint of smoke and a hint, too, of decay. It fills me with nostalgia, but I do not know for what. It is a smell I love, for this is and has always been my favourite season. They said that as I grew older I should recoil from it, the winding down of another year, the descent towards winter, the end of summer pleasures, that I would begin to shift my affections towards spring, when all is looking forward, all is blossoming and greening and sprouting up. But I do not do so. Spring so often promises what in the end it never pays, spring can cheat and lie and disappoint. You can sit at the window and wait for spring many a weary day.

But I have never been let down by autumn, to me it is always beautiful, always rich, it always gives in heaping measure, and sometimes it can stretch on into November, fading, but so gently, so slowly, like a very old person whose dying is protracted but peacefully, in calmness.

And I love the wild days of autumn, the west winds that rock the apple tree and bring down the leaves and fruit and nuts in showers, and the rain after the days of summer dryness. I love the mists and the first frosts that make the ground crisp and whiten the foliage of the winter vegetables.

Soon, perhaps over one wild night, the last of the leaves on our magic apple tree will be sent swirling away, and on the bare branches there will hang here and there the last few, shrivelling fruits, and finally those, too, will thud to the ground and burst open and rot gradually into the soil, or else be taken by the birds, getting hungrier, now that the cold has come, and on that morning, whenever it comes, the autumn will be over.

The Wood

IN EARLY October, the woods begin to come alive again, and that surprises many people, who think of them in autumn as places of decay and dying, falling leaves and animals hiding away for their long winter hibernation. But it is summer there that is the dead time, in summer the air hangs heavy and close and still, nothing flowers, nothing sings, nothing stirs, and no light penetrates.

But, now, there is a stirring, a sense of excitement.

It is morning, not too early, the sun is up and people are about in the lanes. But the air is chilly, and I put on a jacket, and go down the lane, over the stile and through the field. From here, I look down on the shape of Lyke Wood, fitting as snug as an animal in the groin where the two fields that slope towards it meet the Fen. The trees have begun to turn colour but they are all at different stages. In summer in this wood every tree looks much like every other, though of course if you are close up, you can distinguish them by the shape of the leaves, and in the open, where they stand in ones and twos, by the shape of the whole body of the tree. Now though, in decay, the trees have become distinct, separate again, they take back their individual character, for no two species are the same in shading and depth of colour. I stand still and see sulphur-yellow and bright, bright gold, copper and tawny owl's feather brown, sienna and umber and every kind of nut, and the whole pattern breaks like a child's kaleidoscope as a sudden wind blows over the wood, becomes mottled, darker, and then lighter, as the leaves show their backs. The wind dies again.

The dog and I go down, through the gap between the hawthorn

and blackthorn, over the plank laid loosely across the ditch, far beneath which, hidden dark among grasses, a stream flows. Into the wood. Now I see, looking up, that some of the trees still have greenness left, towards the main rib of each leaf, it is only the edges that have yellowed and browned and begun to curl, so that inside the wood we seem to be closer to summer still. And the ash trees have not browned at all. But plenty of leaves have fallen, and there are shafts of light coming through the rents on the roof, it is as though the whole wood were some tumble-down, disused barn, supported on all these tall struts which are the trunks of the trees.

We walk slowly, the dog scuffing and snuffling among the fallen leaves and bracken.

The last time we came here the wood was silent but now it is alive with sounds again, not only the rustle of the falling leaves or the noise the breeze makes stirring the dry branches. There is bird song again, that is the difference, that is what has made the wood seem alive again, and not only the wood, but the garden of Moon Cottage, and the whole countryside around. By the end of last month, the summer silence was over, and now, although there are not many birds in the woods – they have either left on their migratory flight or begun to creep gradually nearer to human habitations again – the ones that are here sing, and their singing lifts the heart.

A week later, we come down to Lyke Wood again, all of us this time. There has been a windy night and, stepping through the hedge gap to go in among the trees, I see at once how much lighter it all is, how much bigger the rents in the roof, there is no sense at all now of a contrast between the sunshine of the fields and the dark shadow of the wood, between one stride and the next. The sunlight is streaming in and, in the sunlight, ash keys and sycamore wings come spinning and twirling, and more and more leaves. They are browner, drier, crisper, Jessica rushes about, her face upturned to the treetops and the open sky shining through them, arms outstretched, trying to catch as many as she can, but just as they are all but in the grasp of her hand, they evade her, give a twist and drift a yard away.

We sit on a fallen beech trunk and watch her, as she and the dog run and stir up piles of golden leaves. He rolls and rolls and then falls accidentally right through one pile into a concealed ditch, like Alice down the rabbit hole, to emerge, stuck all over with burrs and twiggy bits, and Jessica runs in circles, tossing handfuls of leaves up into the air, so that they swirl for a second, catching the sunlight in a shower about her head, and fall again, all over her.

It is a perfect place for the child and the dog, for playing, romping, laughing with laughter that echoes away through the whole wood.

Then, for a moment, the dog goes off somewhere, nose to ground, following a scent, and the child sits down and is quiet, still, and looking up, I see a nuthatch frozen half-way up a tree trunk, where it has been feeding on the insects in the bark, a tiny bird, upside down, slate blue-grey, with a long beak like a needle at the end, and a bright, black eye. It is the eye that has given it away, for it is motionless and well camouflaged against the greyish tree trunk.

I think of how this wood must be at dusk and after dark, owl-full and fox-haunted, alive with the movements of all the night creatures. I should like to come down here then, and sit and watch and listen. I once sat half a summer night in a Dorset wood, waiting to see badgers. It was amazing and frightening, another world, and when they came, the badgers made a noise like earth-moving machinery, crashing through the undergrowth.

On the margin of Lyke Wood, there are plenty of blackthorn bushes but this year hardly a single sloe upon them. I have no idea why that may be, unless it is simply a natural year of recoupment after a previous year's heavy crop. There is wild honeysuckle here, too, rambling around the bushes, and up the deep ditches, showing the last of its pale, buttery flowers, but also bright with berries, ruby-red, gleaming, deadly.

When we reach the top of the slope and the stile again, we look back, and see that the ribs of the wood are showing through at the sides, like those of a starving man, and the grey bones poke upwards to the sky, topped by a last few bunches of dried leaves, like old, curly wigs, and even as we look, the wind rises and blows and tosses the trees about again and more leaves fall.

It is a chill wind, too, for all that the sun is shining, our shadows are already very long, across the yellowed, trodden-down grass. Jessica is carried on her father's shoulders. Up there it is breezier still. She rides as on a howdah, swaying a little from side to side, her hair blowing, and when we walk between the trees up the lane that leads to home, she catches more sycamore keys in her hands, bunches of them, and throws them about, for the joy of seeing them spin.

By the time we reach Moon Cottage the sun has gone behind one puff-ball of mushroom-coloured cloud. We shiver and close the windows. As I do so, I look out and notice that I can see more clearly through the branches of the apple tree, and through all the trees on the far rise beyond Fen Lane, the outlines of here a chimney, there a roof, are beginning to peep through.

Next week when I go down to Lyke Wood again, perhaps to gather kindling, the branches will be completely bare, the whole wood will be open to the sky, full of clear light and having no secrets. Next week, or perhaps the week after, if the wind dies and the last leaves hang on and the sun shines in the middle of the day. For the wood is poised between seasons, no longer a summer wood, certainly, but still half in autumn and reluctant to fall down the last few yards of the slope into real, bare, bitter winter.

Next week. Or the week after. . . .

Cooking

IN THE kitchen, autumn is my favourite season, too, because it is preserving time – jams and jellies, chutneys and pickles, fruit butters and cheeses, and the whole, glorious session rounded off with the making of the mincemeat, to be stored until Christmas.

It is a time for advance preparations and for giving the family plenty of warning, though they get it anyway, when they see the baskets of blackberries, damsons, apples, plums, come into the kitchen. I take a week in the middle of September, when Jessica is safely at school all day and I make a big casserole, and a pot of spaghetti sauce, and put them into the freezer, for suppers, and clear every flat surface I possibly can, ready for work.

Earlier in the month, I walked up to the village notice board and put up a card, begging for the loan or gift of glass jars, because however many I have, full, each year, the wheel only ever seems to come about half-circle again in the form of emptied and returned ones. People in Barley are very good indeed about responding to such notices; within a couple of days, I have been telephoned several times and gone off to collect bicycle baskets full of jars, and carrier bags and boxes of them have appeared anonymously on the doorstep. However many preserves of their own my neighbours want to make, they always manage to find a few empty jars for someone else at the back of a cupboard. These are all scalded, rinsed and dried carefully, and put aside in order of size, and the packets of covers are bought and the sealing rings for the pickle jars replaced.

This year, I kept a record of my preserving week.

Monday

Outside Primrose's gate is a notice, written out by her two daughters, 'Plums for Sale'. I have had my eye on her trees for some while now, and it has looked a good crop, and now they are ready for picking, some, the Victorias with their whitish bloom over the purple, ripe and juicy for immediate eating, others, the smaller yellow ones, still slightly hard and green-tinged. These are the ones I want. They are a bit dull to eat raw, cotton-woolly and rather bland, but perfect for pickling and spicing. Primrose also crystallises a lot each year, for Christmas eating, but having looked at the recipe carefully and realised that I can scarcely leave the plums for ten days, but must attend to them as assiduously as a sick relative, I have opted out of this.

I would be more than happy to buy Primrose's plums but they come free, in exchange for a lot of runner beans that I brought up to her earlier, when mine throve abundantly and hers were late and scanty.

We go up into the small orchard and use a splendid gadget, a sort of wire crown with bag attached, on the end of a long pole; you hook the plums between the points of the crown and they drop into the bag. The lower branches of the plum trees can be stripped by hand, and together we pick twelve pounds, which I take down the lane on the bicycle basket, followed by a long streamer of wasps.

I sort out the plums discarding any that are blemished, wasp-ridden or over-ripe – only a few – wash and dry them. Four pounds are turned into spiced pickled plums which, by winter, will be ready to eat with cold meats, or bread and cheese.

Spiced plums
Choose unblemished fruit, not over-ripe. Wash. Dry. Prick all over with a needle. Pack into bottling jars with wide necks, and, if you can, put a blackcurrant leaf between each layer. Add a few cloves and a cinnamon stick. Boil 1 pint pickling vinegar with 12 oz sugar (demerara for preference) for 5 minutes, until syrupy. Pour over the plums. Cool. Cover tightly. Keep at least 2 months, preferably longer, before serving.

I am not a great maker of jam, simply because we do not eat very much and most of the summer soft fruits we like best eaten fresh.

Plum jam alone is boring, like marrow or rhubarb jams, reminding me of wartime and school teas. But there is a very good, slightly more luxurious variety which I have made this year, and we shall eat on winter Sundays, spread on fresh bread.

Plum, orange and walnut jam

3 lbs plums. 2 oranges. 2½ lbs sugar. 8 oz chopped walnuts. 1 small cup water. Wash and stone the plums. Tie stones in a piece of muslin. Halve oranges, squeeze out the juice, mince the peel. Put all ingredients except sugar and nuts into the preserving pan. Boil, then simmer for 1 hour, stirring occasionally. Meanwhile, warm the sugar in a very low oven, and the jam jars too. Add sugar to the pan gradually. Stir until dissolved. Bring to the boil again, add nuts, stir, boil to setting point, fill jars, seal and cover.

Tuesday

Word has gone round on the village bush telegraph that the High Holt Farm damson tree is ready and anyone is welcome to go and pick as many as they want, so I go, but when I get there, find half a dozen boxes and bowls on a table outside the gate. *Damsons. Please Take.* I do. Mrs Heap, the farmer's wife, sees me and comes out. Apparently this is only the first lot, there will be many more, but her son and his sons were over for the weekend, and they had a merry hour climbing up and pulling down pounds of fruit. She says the tree never has a bad year, but regularly supplies her own needs, and those of her family and anyone in the village who can cope with a lot of damsons. The trees used to be everywhere when I was a child, but have become much scarcer now, because of the ripping-out of so many hedgerows, and because the older trees have died, and young ones are not planted. 'Come back for more, take as many as you like.' But I think I have probably got enough for this year. Damsons are a bit of a bore – *all* those stones, and I do not greatly like the resulting jam. What I do want a good few pounds for is that great Victorian delicacy, Damson Cheese. It is a thick, rich, heavy substance, which we slice and eat with meat, especially cold game. It used to be eaten as a dessert, splendid to behold, elaborately moulded, and served in cut glass dishes, with clotted cream.

Making it is a very messy business, but quite fun. You wash and cover the damsons with water, then simmer them until soft – not very long. Sieve, carefully. (There are *hundreds* of stones.) To each pint of the resulting pulp, add 12 oz sugar, stir until dissolved, then simmer for about 40 minutes or so, stirring often, for it sticks very readily to the bottom of the pan. The mixture should be thick and sticky. Pour into hot jars. The best are small ones with wide necks and straight sides. You can turn the cheese out of these most easily, and use up a relatively small quantity all at once, because once out of its sealed jar it doesn't keep long.

It should be put away for at least three months, and even better six or so, before use. Other fruit cheeses can be made in the same way, apple, gooseberry, bramble. But damson is by far the best and the only one I now bother with, having experimented all round.

Wednesday

It has been a fantastic year for apples. I have never seen so many. Old trees, young trees, orchard trees, garden trees are bent double with every variety of apple, cookers and eaters, red and green. In the markets in the city they are down to twelve or fifteen pence a pound. In the country, they are free, there is a notice on every other gate, everyone is giving them to everyone else, pounds arrive on the doorstep of Moon Cottage daily. The best ones of all come from Louisa's huge old tree that stands outside the garden door of her house. It is a fine sight, and they are *very* fine apples, large, some almost a pound each, light-green, unblemished cookers. I go to pick them and as we sit having a cup of coffee afterwards, in the afternoon sun, more fall all round us and into my basket and on to our heads, and I take so many I have to push the bicycle home up the lane, so precarious is my load on the front. These apples are the kind that store well, so I put a few pounds in a tray with a space between each, wrap them in tissue, and carry them up to the loft. It is dry there, and cool, frost-free with any luck; but the best storing places for apples are lofts under thatch, which Moon Cottage once had.

The rest of the day is spent on the first stage of making savoury jellies. We get through large quantities of these each winter, and the base of them all is plain, apple jelly.

First chop your apples, peel, core, pips and all. This takes ages, but like the chopping of ingredients for chutney is a soothing task. Put into a preserving pan with one pint of water to every 2 lbs of apples, and simmer till soft (time depends on the apples; half an hour to an hour is the guide). Stir and press with a wooden spoon often. This is one reason why preserve-making takes up whole days, with bouts of hard work, and minutes of stirring gently, scattered over long periods of waiting, during which I read a book that doesn't mind being broken into every so often, or write a few letters, or go out to pick some ripe elderberries from the tree on the other side of our garden, for tomorrow. And friends drop in for cups of coffee and wasps are slaughtered and the telephone is answered, and I go outside, just to stand in the sunshine and look about. It is all very pleasant.

When the apple pulp is ready, it goes into that wonderful contraption, the jelly bag. I hang this on a stout hook from the beam over the fireplace and put a giant saucepan underneath it. This will drip away for a good twenty-four hours. During preserving week, it becomes a friendly, familiar sight, full of various fruit pulps. I used to use an old pillow-case slung between the legs of an upside-down wooden stool, but this is a great improvement. Once it is dripping, I take Tinker and a basket, down the lane and over the stile, left across Sheep Hill and into a fringe of rough woodland, on the edge of which are two crab apple trees. Now, oddly enough, they are not at all heavily laden, there are only a few fruits right at the top. Why should that be, when every other apple tree is so heavy? I manage to climb a bit, and get enough crabs to make a few jars of what is the easiest of all jellies, the first one I made, when I began preserving, some years ago. That was when I shared a communal garden in a town, with ten neighbours. Our houses had been built on the site of a much older house, and some of the original trees, including a crab apple, had been left intact. Week by week, I watched from my kitchen window as the fruit reddened and no one took any notice of it. When I went round the houses suggesting tentatively that I might pick it to make crab apple jelly, simply because I couldn't bear to watch it all go to waste on the ground, not only did no one else claim the apples, or object, they came to help. Two young men next door stripped the tree for me from top (and it was high) to bottom, and everyone looked out jars. I made twenty-three pounds of crab apple jelly that year, and all the pulp of it went through that old pillow-case, and it took me a whole week. The neighbours were intrigued and delighted, they had a whip-round for the cost of all the sugar, in return for which I shared out the jelly. The following year, someone else gave me a hand with the chopping and cooking and so the whole thing went on, for seven years, until I moved away. But, by then, they didn't need me, jelly-making was an established, annual neighbourly event.

Thursday
The apple juice is measured and put into the preserving pan, with 1 lb of sugar for every pint, and then two tablespoonsful of lemon juice plus whatever herbs I am using are added. You can make fresh basil, marjoram, thyme, mint, sage or tarragon jelly, adding half a dozen or so sprigs, freshly picked. The jelly is boiled until set, strained and potted. Basil jelly is best of all. It turns a lovely bright red and has a wonderfully subtle flavour.

Thursday is blackberry day. That's because everyone comes out from the city at the weekends to the highways and by-ways to gather brambles, and strip the bushes, at least on all the main lanes, bare of all ripe (and sometimes of plenty of the unripe) fruit. By Thursday, especially if the sun has been shining, more berries have come on, and there are two days to go before the next invasion.

But, fortunately, it *is* only the principal lanes that are visited. Go down Fen Lane, and you will not find a blackberry. Go up the slope to High Holt, on to the ridge and across one field, or else down the lane past Moon Cottage and turn right through one open gateway, and there are hedgerows laden with brambles, and south-facing ones, too, so they are particularly large and juicy and abundant.

This was a difficult year for brambles, I discovered. There were enough, but not so many that I didn't have to work for them. I climbed and clambered and delved, got scratched and stung – that is all part of the job, of course. But, when I wriggled on my stomach under a wooden fence and my jersey became thoroughly entangled in some old barbed wire, it was not so jolly after all. Then several cows came and stared down at me reflectively, and the dog ran in anxious circles, while I went into contortions trying to free myself. I got very hot and cross and then knocked over the basket of fruit, before finally extricating myself by pulling hard – and rending my jumper. Still, as Stanley says when confronted with the thornless, cultivated variety on sale at nursery gardens, 'Brambles should be free – but not easy.'

I make a lot of bramble jelly (which needs some lemon juice to set it, or else you get bramble syrup – though that is very nice, too, poured over ice cream or pies), and then some bramble and apple purée, for the freezer, and then I strip the elderberries off their stalks with a fork and make those into a jelly, with apple and some blackberries. Elderberries are an underrated hedgerow fruit, loved by the birds, but very little picked by people, except for wine-making. They have a peculiar flavour and a little goes a long way but it is worth acquiring a taste for, and the colour of the jelly and jam is wonderful, a dark, ruby red.

At the end of this day, I am stung, scratched, sore and stained, and the kitchen smells marvellous. There are rows of glowing jars on the dresser shelves, like so many jewels, deep red, orange, burgundy, pale pink, pale green, purple-black. I label them, before carrying them upstairs to the store cupboard, which is in our bedroom, and there, when I have lined them up, I gaze in deep satisfaction, I feel as if we shall indeed be 'preserved' against the ravages of this coming winter, and go off to have a long, hot, soothing bath.

Friday

Chutney day. I begin very early indeed, as soon as the family have gone. Outside, it has turned grey and cold and drizzly. I put on the lights and some good, food-for-thought programmes on the wireless and begin to slice and chop, onions, apples, green tomatoes, and to weigh out brown sugar and sultanas and raisins, and to measure spoonfuls of ginger and salt, cloves and cinnamon, mustard and cayenne pepper. Chutney-making gives the kitchen an entirely different smell today, vinegary, spicy, pungent, causing me to catch my breath, and wipe watering eyes.

I made three kinds. Apple, which was a success, green tomato, which was very dull, and elderberry chutney; we ate the first jar of that too soon and it was very odd, and much too 'raw'. I then put it to the back of the cupboard and found it again recently – that is, a whole year and a bit later. It was amazingly delicious – but still odd.

There are plenty of easily obtainable recipes for apple chutney, combined with various things, but mainly raisins, onions and perhaps tomatoes, too, along with the usual spices, vinegar and sugar; the best thing about chutney-cooking is that you can play around with the ingredients a bit, according to what you have most of (so long as you use the right quantities of vinegar and sugar) and change the spices ad lib, so that you create your own personal recipe, and it changes a bit from year to year.

Elderberry Chutney
4 pints elderberries (The best are the ripest and they always grow highest!)
8 oz seedless raisins
8 oz dark brown sugar
6 oz onions
1 oz salt
cayenne pepper, mace and allspice
2 pints vinegar (cider vinegar is nice, malt will do fine)
Put everything into a preserving pan and stir over a low heat until the sugar is dissolved. Cook for ages, stirring now and then, until it is all soft and thick and sticky – but not sticking to the pan. Spoon into warm jars. Seal with plastic lids (not paper, the vinegar evaporates gradually, and the chutney dries out and goes hard and

shrunken; not metal, the vinegar eats into and corrodes it).

In the middle of the chutney-making, Jane telephoned. Would I like some quinces? She had a lot, ripe, on the bush, but she has broken her arm and doesn't feel up to doing any preserving this year. If I can pick them I am welcome to them *and* she has some jars for me, too.

The only recipes I have for quinces are for jam, and I'm not sure I want the bother of making it, at this stage, but nor do I want to pass up the fruit, which is so interesting and unusual in flavour. When I get to Jane's house, a short walk up the lane, she has not only quinces and jars but a recipe for preserved quinces, which you eat cold, with thick, clotted cream, as a very rich dessert. So I bring everything home and, while the chutney is simmering in the pan, make preserved quinces in another. It is very easy indeed, and they are very good, though they don't keep long and you can't eat many at once, because they are *very* sweet. I put them on slices of sponge cake and let the juices soak in, before serving.

5 lb quinces

1½ pints cold water

3 lb sugar

Peel, quarter and core the fruit and drop the pieces straight into cold water. Boil peelings and cores in water for 15 minutes. Add the quinces to the liquid you have strained from the peelings. Cook very slowly until tender. Remove quinces with a slotted spoon. Add sugar to the liquid that remains in the pan. Stir until dissolved, then boil. Add quinces. Cook until the liquid is clear. Put into warmed jars, cover and seal.

Saturday

Mincemeat day. And the kitchen smells of Christmas. As you don't have to do any cooking of mincemeat, Jessica can help me and does so with glee. She has a wooden board and a sharp knife and helps me to chop the apples, the crystallized ginger, and glacé cherries, while I do the lemon and orange peel and the nuts, and then we weigh out suet and raisins and brown sugar, and spoon out the spices, and put everything into a vast mixing bowl, and pour over the brandy, and then we stir and stir and stir, until our arms ache, and Stanley comes in and has a stir, too.

Then he and Jessica go out for a walk with the dog, and I pack down the brown, fruity, spicy goo into jars, and cover them and take them up to the store cupboard.

Then, I wash up the preserving pan, bowls, knives and wooden spoons, and put them all away until next autumn, and make a pot of tea, and sit feeling entirely contented, and rather smug.

Over the next months, the jars of jelly and jam and chutney will be opened and eaten, and given away to friends for Christmas, and taken as contributions to the harvest festival and the W.I. autumn produce sale and the school Christmas bazaar, and I shall feel glad that at least some of the fruits of the garden and the hedgerows have been put to the best of use.

The Garden

I LIKE autumn in the garden. I like the way it smells, when I'm working there, and the satisfaction of harvesting the crops and storing them away. I like digging, if the soil is not too hard or water-logged. I like piling up all the spent foliage of the finished crops on the new compost heap and taking the cover off the one that has been rotting down through the summer months, to find out whether it is the proper, crumbly, friable consistency – or not. Composting is a good activity, but I have certainly not found it so straightforward or foolproof as all the books and magazine articles make out. The first heap I ever made got too wet at once and was simply black and brown lumps of completely undigested waste, of use to neither man nor beast. It smelled foul, too. Then I realised that I was building the heap too slowly. Then, I was not using any activator, such as manure, or soil, or a sprinkling of sulphate of ammonia. Then, I put in far too many grass cuttings and got silage instead of compost. The next heap was far too dry and didn't rot properly, either. I had begun by using a wire basket on the soil and covering the finished heap with black polythene, weighted down with big stones. But, in the end, I bought one of the large, specially-manufactured plastic bins, with holes at the sides, and an airtight top of capillary matting, crowned with a close-fitting lid. I incorporated some chicken manure and a little of their bedding straw, too, to serve as an activator, and the whole thing began to steam like a hayrick within a few days, and broke down to beautiful compost within six weeks. I shall never make enough to enrich the whole garden, simply because we are too small a family to have enough kitchen vegetable waste, and the garden is in turn not big enough to supply vast quantities of clippings, and so forth, but if I can incorporate at least a couple of bins a year, it will help the heavy clay immeasurably. Fortunately, the orchard garden soil is so rich, with the leaf mould of years, that it needs nothing at all, and will not do so for some time to come.

In early autumn, there are still plenty of vegetables to pick in the kitchen garden of the cottage, partly because I tend to sow and plant everything rather late, and also because the September weather this year went on being summery and settled, dry and hot, though with plenty of heavy dews night and morning, to provide the ground with some moisture.

The peas were finished early, and I could not honestly say that I had a heavy or successful crop at all, but the few pounds we did get were so delicious, it was worth all the effort. The dwarf French beans, after their bad start, went happily on and on, both the green and the wonderful purple variety, which never have any fibre in them, even if they are missed, and allowed to grow huge. The courgettes were abundant, too. Their plants grew to two or three feet high, and it was difficult to get at the fruits, so protected were they under the umbrella-like leaves, and tangled, very prickly stems, and we also had to be careful not to grasp hold of a flower and a bee feeding off the pollen within it at the same time. It seems to attract them very strongly.

The spinach did well in the orchard garden, but not so well by the cottage, partly, I think, because the hens found it a couple of times, but probably because the soil was too heavy for it to thrive.

The best crop of all has been the runner bean. Looking up at the eight feet or so of densely tangled foliage, thick stems and tendrils, I could well understand how the story of Jack and the Beanstalk came to be told, for you could easily believe in the possibility of these beans climbing to the sky, given half a chance, *and* being strong enough to bear the weight of a boy. The canes were having a hard time staying upright, and after one or two windy nights I had to haul the whole frame erect again, after it had fallen sideways.

I picked runner beans every other day, at least three and often five or six pounds at a time, and tried not to let them grow too long and thick and coarse – eight inches is the very most they should be, and no more than half an inch thick. I am horrified at the great, huge, husky things for sale in the market; they will have a bitter flavour, and be hairy and very fibrous and require a lot of tedious stringing.

Very young, slender runner beans are almost as good as asparagus, steamed for a short while and eaten with melted butter, but they do freeze better than many vegetables, again, if picked young, and frozen immediately afterwards. They must be blanched, for a couple of minutes, though this is one of the most boring of kitchen jobs, and when they are cooked subsequently, they will not need very long in the water or steam.

One of the horrors of childhood food was runner beans, cut crossways but still thick and stringy, boiled for ages, and then covered in a gooey, savoury white sauce, and served with fatty shoulder of lamb – at school, I hasten to add, not by my mother, who was a good, plain but sensitive cook.

I enjoy walking across the field in the morning, in wellingtons that get soaking wet the moment I step on to the grass, and standing under the bean frame picking, stretching as far as I can to reach the ones at the top, and being wary of the bees droning in and out of the scarlet flowers. In the end, I had to take across a short pair of kitchen steps to reach the top beans, and although it is a bit perilous, once up there, I can look out over the garden and down the field beyond the hawthorn hedge, just as far as the top of the trees in Lyke Wood. What a place for a kitchen garden!

The rows of celeriac are looking fine by the middle of September, the tops a rich, dark green, and pretty too, feathery, and smelling aromatically of celery if you pull a bit off and crush it between finger and thumb. The bulbs are swelling up nicely, resting almost on top of the soil surface. They need a great deal of water and a liquid feed once a week, too, and in dry spells I have spent half an hour a day doing all this, but if I do not, the bulbs are shrivelled and small and disappointing.

The sprouting broccoli is full of little holes, which mean cater-pillars, so I have to go round picking them off every morning and evening, and if they become too invasive, shall have to resort to the spray.

The asparagus foliage is beautiful, graceful and delicate, and I can see why flower arrangers always want to steal it, but they are kept at bay. In November, it is beginning to go yellow and to shrivel and must be cut down, and the whole bed covered in soil and, if possible, some seaweed – failing that, well-rotted manure.

The globe artichokes, those other, handsome plants, with their spreading, spiky leaves, will have to be cut down and protected against the frosts, too. We have had half a dozen artichokes off the plants in their first year, which was a bonus, for I had not expected any until next summer. They were tender and smallish, and the first couple we cooked for too long, so that they were a bit watery.

The orchard garden, with its variety of plants, has been a joy to look at all the year, and there is less work to do there, on the permanent crops, than in the rest of the garden, though we have had a lot of trouble with creeping weeds, bindweed and nettles, and have had to carry a lot of water to and fro.

Gradually, the summer vegetable crops are finished and the patches of ground exposed, gradually, I try and dig them over and spread some early manure and compost, rather than leave it all to be worked at once, later.

Earlier, as I came out of the kitchen door and looked down the garden, all was green and spreading and climbing. Now, towards the end of September, the plot looks smaller and flatter, as the tall peas and beans have come down, and the colour you see most is earth-brown.

In the other gardens of the village, onions are being pulled up and dried in the mid-day sunshine, and then plaited and hung up to store, and carrots and parsnips are being put into trays of sand, potatoes into clamps; beans and peas are down and the canes and sticks stored in sheds, rubbish is piled in heaps and everywhere the bonfires begin again, the early morning mist is smoky-smelling in

October. Our own bonfire is smouldering, too, a slow, quiet sort, of garden refuse and tidyings that can't be composted, and some household paper and rubbish for padding out, and bits of straw and string, the thin line of smoke wanders over the wall and away down the Buttercup field.

I am ashamed of the flower garden. When all the rest of Barley is ablaze with orange and scarlet and yellow and gold, dahlias and chrysanthemums in all their glory, my refusal to spend much time or take a lot of trouble over flowers comes home to roost. The sunflowers that did succeed in growing up are magnificent, three of them are nine feet high and upturning their bright faces and shaggy heads to the sun, and there is a straggle of Michaelmas daisies over by the wall, a few late roses, one or two second-flowering yellow daisies. Otherwise, everything is a scruff of seedling hollyhock grown too tall, straggling, leggy, flowerless wallflowers that should have been taken up, and phlox, all dead-heads and floppy stems, and not much else.

Mr Spooner calls me over, as I walk up the lane to pick damsons again. Do I want any plants? He has dozens, in neat rows, and I am more than welcome. There are aquilegia, sweet williams, delphiniums, lupins, wallflowers. . . . I don't deserve such bounty, but I accept them all gratefully, and determine that I shall not let him down. His own garden is always so fine, a riot of colour from one end of the year to the next, organised, old-fashioned, cared-for.

Next year, I am going to try and grow dahlias, in spite of the fact that they attract ear-wigs and so are not pleasant to have in the house, and that you have to remember to take up and store the tubers before the first frosts and to re-plant them the following year. For dahlias give a jewel-like glow to the heart of the autumn garden, they are, in a mass, so resplendent. I always envy them when I see them. I envy Mr Elder's prize chrysanthemums, too, those cup-winning puffballs, but I would never in a hundred years have time or patience or motivation to grow them, they are hand-reared in the way that children or puppies are, and can't be left for two minutes together, for fear some disaster will strike. But, if I cannot manage a few dahlias, and rear the plants Mr Spooner has given me, it will be a poor show.

One day, at the end of October, it was almost summer, still, warm and with a clear blue sky. Then, overnight, the clouds blew up from the west, it turned dank and chill and drear, the lights went on earlier, the gardens dripped and the last of the leaves and apples hung, sodden and sorry, on the little tree. I turned my mind to fruit trees. A new area of Albert Baker's orchard was cleared and I made a plan, then went to collect a lot of the bushes I had ordered. I should eventually like to have half a dozen apple trees, on the dwarf rootstock, M27, to form a natural boundary line to my part of this old garden, but for this year, I am planting only softer fruits, on bushes.

There are three rows of raspberry canes, of the old variety called Lloyd George. It was hard to find them, but eventually, as so often in the friendly, helpful community of gardeners, someone told me of someone who knew a person who . . . and I got them. I have backed these up with a commoner, mid-season variety, but in the autumn garden I have decided not to bother with autumn-fruiting raspberries. Their yield is comparatively poor, and the fruits tend to be hard to pick, and to pull off the centre core without breaking.

I dug in a large quantity of well-rotted chicken manure before planting the blackcurrant bushes and decided on a later-flowering variety, because in the past few years we have had such cold springs, and most of my neighbours seem to have lost crop after crop, when a very late frost or even a hailstorm has pinched and dashed off all the blossom. As well as black and redcurrants, I have put in a couple of bushes of white, mainly because nobody much seems to grow them now, and I feel they need support, if they are not to become extinct. Also, they are delicious, in pies, and to augment the other currants in jelly.

The gooseberries are all Leveller. This variety produces big, golden almost plum-like dessert fruit, that doesn't need much, if any, cooking, but they do need a very rich, fertile soil, and a sheltered site, which is exactly what they have got, here in the orchard.

There will be a lot of work indeed, in spraying against aphids, and in mulching, and picking and pruning all this fruit, and there will also be one major financial outlay – we shall have to provide a netting cage against the depredations of the birds. I do loathe the sight of these and they cost a fortune: the old gardening men I knew in my childhood didn't have such luxuries, they used bird-scarers, but in the orchard garden, where there are not many comings and goings to disturb them, and a great many trees and bushes and hedges in which they can hide, the birds would strip the fruit crops in a couple of days. Cages it will have to be.

Autumn is bulb-planting time again, and I get out the bowls and pots, and buy some fibre, and then get crocuses and snowdrops nicely buried, and put into the dark cupboard until Christmas. I shall also do some sweet-smelling hyacinths, though I have often found they are either in too warm a room, and grow on huge, etiolated stems which flop over, or they are too cold, and do not come on at all. They are worth the effort, though, especially the pure white kinds.

In autumn, too, everyone is dividing plants, so a walk round a few houses in the village means I can beg this and that in exchange for something of my own. This year, as well as aquilegia, I am after some of the lily-like flowers called hemerocallis, which look graceful in the garden, and last for weeks and weeks in the house.

I have also bought a cold-frame. I wanted to acquire a good, second-hand, old-fashioned wooden one, like the cucumber frame into which Bill the lizard fell in *Alice in Wonderland*, but my search was unrewarded, so the one we bought eventually is aluminium – but with glass, not ugly corrugated plastic. Into this are going some lettuce for next spring, and some sweet peas, to see if I can get them off to a good start. In the spring, I shall put in peat pot sowings of French and runner beans, because I should like to manage at least one crop earlier than I usually achieve.

Village Life

ALL THROUGH the afternoon of the last Tuesday in September, the lane leading up from Moon Cottage, to the church and the W.I. hall, is busy; cars arrive, and their boots are opened and unloaded, bicycles, their baskets full, wobble along, and stop, very suddenly, and their riders emerge above piled-up foliage and flowers. People walk slowly, carrying cake-tins piled on top of each other.

Inside the hall, the trestle-tables have been set up, everything is put behind and in front of them, and on top and underneath and, finally, anywhere at all on the floor. Three volunteers are checking everything in, making sure price labels are clearly and securely attached, and later three other members arrive, the hostesses for the evening, with biscuits and cakes and sandwiches, bridge-rolls, sausages, savoury flans cut into individual squares, tarts full of the new season's jam and lemon curd. The urn is lugged out of its cupboard, the cups and saucers and spoons are set out on another table.

Tonight is the W.I. autumn produce Bring and Buy Sale, one of the highlights of the year, tonight, there is a full house apart from the two members who are in hospital, and the one who has a new baby and the one who has gone to the United States for six months. There is a feeling that the year has begun again, that we are re-assembled safely, from holidays all over this country and the rest, and having families home all summer and friends to stay, ready to get on with the winter of meetings and talks and activities. It's a good atmosphere, positive, cheerful.

As I walk up the lane just before seven o'clock, I realise that this is the last time it will still be at all light on a W.I. night, for Summer Time ends next week. But I don't mind. I have tired of summer, it is time things began again. I like the sense of conviviality and community, among such a disparate crowd of women.

The hall is transformed. The tables are arranged in a square, in the middle of which stand the members who are doing the selling for this evening. Everyone else is milling around, hanging up coats, clutching purses, eyeing the display, anxious for the start. The produce sale is rather like the sort of weekly market at which country women can rent a stall and sell whatever produce they have available, through the year, but this one is in aid of W.I. funds, not of individuals. We need funds. There is the electricity bill, the cost of speakers, the contribution to the county office, the price of tea. . . .

There are flowers, divided into bunches and wrapped in wet newspaper, wonderful dahlias from Mrs Streetly and Mrs Spooner and Mrs Plum, some late, dark red roses, tightly packed together, orange and bronze and white chrysanthemums on tall woody stems, the sort you have to crush with a hammer before you can put them in water. There are plant clumps which have been divided, too, alchemilla mollis, the flower arranger's delight, which I cannot get rid of from the garden of Moon Cottage, so invasive is it, but which others prize and covet, for its beauty when covered with thousands of water-drops, from dew or rain, caught like diamonds on a pin-cushion. There are old-fashioned clovey pinks, and variegated hostas, and ground cover plants, the yellow St John's Wort, of which Miss Alder has a hedge so thick it looks like yards of bright cloth, when in full flower, in June. Here are some aquilegia, which I ear-mark quickly, and a lot of lamium (decorative dead-nettle, also too invasive for my liking), and clumps of primulas, here is a giant bag of King Alfred daffodil bulbs, and gnarled tubers of iris.

Mrs Plum has the vegetable table, the baskets of potatoes and carrots and parsnips and onions, the pounds and pounds and pounds of runner beans and French beans, which surely no one can want to buy, for everyone has brought some to sell. I have put up three pounds of my dwarf burgundy French beans, and there they lie, purple as grapes. Everyone looks at them suspiciously. There is a basket of cobnuts and another of field mushrooms and a third of dark damsons. There are a good many cabbages and the first of the celery, with clumps of sooty soil still clinging to the bottom. There are a lot of tomatoes, and they are all very ripe; it was a wonderful summer for them, in greenhouses and out of doors. One or two ridge cucumbers lie next to marrows, and Lavender has sent the largest pumpkin I have ever seen. Everyone admires it and no one knows quite what they would do with it, if they were to buy it.

On the adjacent table are the cakes and pastries, in bags and on plates, and there is some bread, too, and all of this is sold in no time at all, because home-made cakes are unbeatable, they always sell, at bazaars and sales everywhere. I buy a pineapple upside-down cake gleaming with stickiness on top, and a sponge cake iced by Miss Alder with the sort of painstaking care that I would never have patience to devote, all whorls and curls and rosettes. There are flapjacks and oatcakes and loaves of date and walnut and malt bread, all the wholesome colours of good baking, and chocolate brownies and spiced biscuits and cherry buns and Florentines, and two precious bags of Jane's doughnuts, very tiny, very light, dusted in sugar and made that afternoon. These are fought over by seven ladies, and there is such dissent that in the end the President confiscates them and lots are drawn. I do not win. I think, inwardly, that the member who does has the sort of figure that has been acquired by winning just such bags of doughnuts for years. There is another draw, for a magnificent fruit torte, all layers of raspberries and cream and hazelnut sponge, a work of art.

The jars of preserves go the rounds. In a sort of elaborate dance, I buy Mrs Plum's date and banana chutney and she buys my basil jelly and Lavender buys Mrs Lightly's marmalade and she buys Lavender's lemon curd and we all buy a bottle of Miss Moor's blackcurrant cordial, made from a recipe of her great-grandmother's, which she will not divulge, and out of the fruit from her own, rambling orchard. Miss Moor is a remarkable lady. She is not very old, perhaps in her mid-sixties, but she is badly crippled with rheumatoid arthritis, and walks with the help of a frame and cannot hear terribly well. Five years ago, her sister, with whom she had lived as contentedly and devotedly as could be imagined, was killed when the dustcart crushed her against the wall outside their cottage. That was Miss Ivy Moor. The survivor is Miss Holly. As a result of the shock, Miss Holly's hair all fell out, and now she wears a not-very-good wig, perhaps resembling the colour she remembers her hair to have been when she was a girl, rather orangey-brown. She is famous for her embroidery, which has been used on vestments for the Cathedral, and processional banners; she used to rescue old donkeys, when she was younger, and her sister was alive, but the supply dried up and, besides, she could not manage them on her own, crippled as she is. So she rescues cats, and feeds the birds, and her garden is a wilderness and a paradise for both in an odd sort of mutual harmony, and there, also, she has old shrub roses and wild honeysuckle clambering up the trunks of the fruit trees, and a muddle of herbaceous and wild flowers everywhere. And the few remaining fruit bushes, from which she manages to pick enough currants for her cordials. Miss Moor drives about in a three-wheeled, invalid motor car, and makes lemonade and wonderful brandied pears and peaches, and pot-pourri and fudge and ginger-beer and lavender bags, all of which, like the syrups, she gives away to children and to bazaars and to neighbours and to the W.I. As a young woman, she used to play the harp, and is said to keep it still in her attic, and to finger it nostalgically on moonlit nights, but that I do not believe.

There is the Branch Secretary's cinder toffee on sale, next to Miss Holly Moor's walnut fudge, so I buy some of both, and a big jar of pickled onions, as well as the cakes and preserves and the plants and a bunch of blood- and flame- and fire-coloured dahlias.

The hall sounds like the inside of a parrot show, and the money is chinking into the old tobacco tins and then the tea urn begins to whistle and steam and everything is sold, and we are called to order, to stand and sing 'Jerusalem', the Women's Institute hymn, and then to listen to a few notices, before we break up again for the refreshments. 'Jerusalem' is an anachronism, it makes me laugh to think that we sing it at all, and to wonder what Blake would have made of it, and it takes me back to my youth, too, for it was my school song. I would have expected to be deeply embarrassed, singing it again in adult life, among a lot of village women, accompanied by a slightly out-of-tune piano. Oddly enough, when it comes to it, I never am.

I look around the room at everyone. Friends. Neighbours. Grey-haired, lined and wrinkled faces, middle-aged faces, beginning to sag, the faces of young women. Most are married, some not. There are working wives of farmers, there are gardeners. None of us has manicured and lily-white hands. Otherwise, we are all very different. From different generations and backgrounds – different social classes, too, let it be said, for, having been said, it can be dismissed, it simply doesn't matter. There are women who use their brains in their daily jobs, work in the university city whose spires you see as you drop down the last hill of the village beyond Barley, there are the wives of dons and doctors and clergymen, women who have young children, women who have great-grandchildren; women whose ancestors have been buried in Barley churchyard for genera-tions back, and women, like me, who have scarcely lived here any time at all, but who feel at home, because we have at once been made welcome.

The W.I. is a good institution. It is not only about jam- and cake-making, though it *is* about those things, and so it should be, for they are good activities, at a premium now more than ever before, in a fast-moving, mechanised, society; it is about tea-drinking and exchanging recipes, then, and garden plants and knitting patterns, too. But it is not smug or mindless, inward-looking or narrow-minded. It is what each village makes it. It expresses, by its very existence and strength for so many years, a very great many of the important concerns of all kinds of women, and women make up more than half the population, after all. It has a voice, it carries weight, it cares about national and international issues, matters of life and death and health and sickness, of community care and survival, of the upbringing of the young and the welfare of the old.

Politicians and policy-makers, law-givers and public bodies and Royal Commissions, all take serious notice of the collective resolutions of the W.I. on many important matters. It is a body without religious or political affiliations, viewpoint or bias, but that is not to say that it contents itself with comments only on uncontroversial, trivial or domestic issues. And what it agrees and proclaims on a national level has been decided all the way down by the vote of each member of each branch. If I see any faults in its structure, and in its organisation, it is in the proliferation of committees and their officers, and a certain rigidity in the hierarchical outlook at the top. But there are some women, just as there are plenty of men, who like to spend their time – and it is voluntary time – on committees and in meetings, passing resolutions. It's a harmless enough activity, I suppose, and no one is obliged to follow suit at branch level.

The only W.I. branch I know is that in Barley. It is friendly, informal, not too high-powered, but by no means, therefore, frivolous in its activities. There are a lot of good talks, on travel, on country life and conservation, on crafts, on the local past. There is drinkable tea and excellent home-made refreshments, and conversation which is sometimes gossip, but not only gossip, and when it is, I have never noticed that it is backbiting or malicious.

For any women newly arrived in a village community, it is an ideal way of getting to know neighbours and turning them into friends. For many older women, perhaps without any transport, perhaps semi-invalid, and sometimes living alone, it is the only social occasion in the month; for the busy ones, still at work, in the village, on the farm, in the home and garden, or else in the world outside, it is a haven, to come to for relaxation, conviviality, refreshment, and for a view, in whatever the talk may be on any evening, of a new activity, or a different world.

All this I thought, as I looked round the room that September evening, at Mrs Plum and Mrs Streetly, at Primrose and Lavender and Jane, at Miss Holly Moor and Miss Dale, and the parson's sister and Lady P, who is in her twenties, and Lady D who is over eighty, and Mrs Meadow, whose house dates from the time of King Henry VII, and Mrs Brown, who lives in the smallest cottage imaginable, one up and two down, with a tiny kitchen and bathroom extension out back. Mrs Brown's front door opens not, as you would expect, on to her sitting room but on to a long narrow passage between her two rooms, and beyond it, through an archway, is the garden, small and square and packed as pins in a pin-cushion with plants and vegetables and fruit, the whole bordered on all sides, and down each side of the garden path, by a perfect, foot-high box hedge, clipped absolutely smooth and even and square. I like to hover about in the lane, hoping that Mrs Brown will open her door, for a glimpse down that dark tunnel towards the garden beyond is like a glimpse into a magical world, the world that Alice saw when she opened the door and put one eye to it and saw the garden of flowers beyond.

At the end of the evening, the tables are cleared, everything has been sold, except the pumpkin and my purple beans. I feel rather badly about this. What is wrong with them? Nothing, they taste delicious. 'Yes, dear,' says vague Mrs Streetly, 'but beans ought to be *green*, oughtn't they?'

I take my basket full of produce bought and beans unsold, and go home down the lane with the others. We do not need our torches and lanterns, there is a full moon. The air smells cool and sweet and fresh. One by one, my friends go through doors and down driveways and up front paths, calling, Goodnight, Goodnight.

*

Autumn-time is apple-time and apples make cider. It is the end of October. Time to pay a visit to the Twomeys.

The Twomeys do not live in Barley, strictly speaking their farm is in the next parish, at Linton St Leonard, but it always seems to me as if it exists in some other world entirely, the Twomeys and their amazing place are creatures from some crazy, surrealistic storybook, from a past that never was and a present that cannot possibly be. I often wonder, moreover, if The Authorities know about the Twomeys.

You drive out of Barley on the Linton road, past Cross Gallows and the Long Barn, for about four miles, drop down an abrupt dip between conifers, climb up steeply again and, just as the car is groaning and straining in second gear and almost at the top, there is a concealed entrance between overgrown, overhanging bushes to the left, into which you swing, over a rusty cattle-grid and then along what is not a driveway, not a road, but a messy cinder track, which broadens out, just as you leave the trees, into a piece of grass-overgrown, open yard-cum-field. In front of you is the small, four-square stone farmhouse, all around are the outbuildings, barns, stables, sties, sheds, and all in the most appalling state of disrepair.Corrugated tin roofs hang askew and have gone rusty or else have grass and weeds growing out of them, slates and tiles have slipped and fallen, roofs are bowing in the middle, doors swing open on broken hinges, or are propped up with old cans and stakes. The house, which might once upon a time have been rather nice, neat and plain and sensible, pleasing to the eye, is a sorry sight of peeling paint work and tatty curtains and the odd boarded-up window pane. You could be forgiven for thinking the place was empty and completely fallen into disuse.

Once, there were animals here, cattle, horses, pigs, fowl. Now, there are none. The Twomeys gave up keeping animals more than ten years ago, though they still go to market, regular as clockwork. No one knows why. No one knows how old they are, either, but they can't be far off seventy, and maybe they are much more. They have that timeless, old-young look peculiar to babies, orientals, very old men and creatures out of science fiction and fantasy.

The Twomeys are brothers, not actually twins, but as near as makes no difference, for they look more or less alike, and what they look like are, roughly, Tweedledum and Tweedledee. What their Christian names are I do not know. I doubt if anyone does, except they themselves. They are universally known as 'Twomeys', and each of them is addressed to his face as Mr Twomey by everyone, and they call each other nothing but 'He'.

Today, I park on the grass and walk around the back of the house. It is very quiet here, apart from the constant raucous crying of the rooks that flock in the belt of dead elms over to the bottom of the far field. I knock on the back door of the farmhouse first. It is slightly ajar. I peer in, but there is only dimness, and a smell. God knows what it is like inside Twomeys'. No one has ever been. It has been owned by them, and their father and grandfather and great-grandfather before them, way back, and, everyone says, never cleaned out in all that time. That's what everyone *says*. But it might be clean as a pin for all they actually know. I doubt it, though. As they keep their out-buildings, and their persons, and as, by all accounts, they used to keep their animals, so they doubtless keep their living quarters. A row of old plant pots full of dead, dried-up geraniums, interlaced with cobwebs and flies, stands on the kitchen window-sill, and outside, a tap has been dripping down on to the stone below for many a year, so that the whole thing is slimed over thickly with green.

I walk over to the big building, a cross between a barn, a garage and a shed. 'Mr Twomey!'

Eventually, one of them, I don't know which, emerges, and just behind him stands the other. They look quite pleased to see me, they grin and nod and bob and look at each other furtively and roll their eyes. This is a characteristic of the Twomeys, they are never still. They remind me of those fat, bald toys with loose eyes and rounded bases that babies have, and which, when pushed, rock over and back, over and back, eyes revolving. The Twomeys rock to and fro on their heels now.

One of them is a fraction taller than the other and he is the one who never starts a sentence. His brother never finishes one, so you talk to the two of them in concert, glancing uneasily between. They have little round heads without much hair left on them and round pot bellies hanging over their trouser tops. They wear collarless grey shirts, corduroy trousers with braces and boots, and they may have worn these same clothes night and day since they first grew into them.

'How are you?' I ask brightly.

'Oh yes, oh yes, oh yes, very. . .'

'. . . well, thank you, oh yes, very well, very. . .'

'Is there any cider yet?'

'Oh yes, oh yes, oh yes. . .'

'. . .yes, oh, cider, oh yes, cider's ready, oh yes.'

That is how they talk, interweaving their phrases like singers of a fugue, and as they speak they grin and reveal odd teeth here and there, with gaps between, and as they grin they twitch, and roll their eyes and rock back on their heels and exchange glances.

Everyone agrees that it is best not to inquire or to speculate too closely as to what exactly goes into Twomeys' cider, locally known, as the brothers themselves are known, as just 'Twomeys'. Huge wooden vats stand open in the great shed, and stories go that bats drop in and rats climb up and fall over the edge and decompose and it all adds to the flavour of the scrumpy. I don't know. But it tastes wonderful, mellow and still and smooth, and it packs a kick like an old mule.

The Twomeys have an old pick-up truck which they drive about the countryside from farm to farm, private house to smallholding, buying up apples. They do have a few trees of their own, but nothing like enough to supply the quantity they require. If you have an apple tree or trees and can't, or don't want to, use the fruit, and do want to make 'a few bob', you call up Twomeys, and along they come. They are, I am told, extremely astute business-men. They buy cheaply and make their cider for virtually nothing and sell it at a profit which is compounded, everyone is certain, by being undeclared and tax-free, for the Twomeys do not advertise their produce, not by so much as a hand-chalked board on the side of the road, all their business comes by word of mouth. People drive for miles to get Twomeys'.

You have to bring your own receptacle, barrel or jug or old demi-john, otherwise you must risk taking away the cider in unmarked polythene containers with handles which are lying around the Twomeys' yard, and doubtless once contained tractor oil or disinfectant.

You would think, indeed, that we'd all be poisoned by drinking Twomeys but, so far as I know, no one ever has been.

I take along two gallon jars and pay, and one of them pockets the cash in his baggy corduroys, nodding and rolling the while, and the other disappears into the barn and comes back after a few minutes with my scrumpy. Rumour has it that, as Twomeys have never been seen to go to the bank, and when they visit the post office it is only to collect their pensions, never to pay anything into a savings account, they have socks or old mattresses upstairs in the ramshackle farmhouse, stuffed with money. Rumour has an awful lot of things, about Twomeys.

They seem to be supremely contented men, needing nothing and no one, neither wife nor child, friend or neighbour, only each other. Most of the time I let myself think what everyone else thinks about them, that they are immortal. Certainly they don't fit into the twentieth century, or into any other century, for that matter. They never go away, have no television set, they do not take a newspaper. I wonder what they do do? I also wonder, from time to time, what will happen to the survivor when the first brother dies, for they seem to be inextricably inter-dependent, like Siamese twins, or the face and obverse of some coin. And what will happen to their premises – where cider-making is the only activity and everything is so fallen into decay and disuse? Who will they leave it to?

I said all this to Mr Elder, the evening after I'd collected the scrumpy. He sniffed. 'Them,' he said. 'Don't you fret about them. They'll have something up their sleeve, never you worry.'

Perhaps. Anyway, I liked the fact that he apportioned one sleeve between the two of them.

There could scarcely be a greater contrast than between the Twomeys and the Hon. Claudia Hay, and yet they have a certain separateness and independence in common, she is her own mistress in the same way as they are their own masters, answerable to no parent, spouse, or employer. She, like them, is doing exactly as she pleases in the way she decides, she is similarly different and set apart and speculated about in the villages around, and there is something about her that is unknowable and impenetrable, as there is about the two cider-brewing brothers on their derelict farm.

Claudia lives in the opposite direction, across the fields a mile to the East of Lyke Wood, a good way out of the village, and next door to no one. To her right is the wood, to her left and all around and behind her the Fen, ahead the slopes up to Barley.

I first met her when I was out with the dog and she was coming towards me with a pair of pigeons in one hand, a gun under her arm, and a golden retriever nuzzling her heels. Tinker went up to the dog at once and bounded about and nosed around, while I called him away and whistled and he took absolutely no notice. She, meanwhile, had ordered the retriever quietly to heel and to heel it had gone, and there remained, and for all the notice it took of Tinker he might have been invisible. I am always impressed by a perfectly trained dog and said as much, as I paused, apologising for mine, and simultaneously trying to grab his collar. In fact, he was doing no harm at all, but I was anxious to demonstrate that I had some degree of control – as indeed I do, when the dog decides to concede it to me. 'Look at that,' I said, admiring the retriever, 'that's obedience for you.' 'It is,' she said, and strode on. But, then, she turned and called over her shoulder, 'I know who *you* are.'

And went. I found that disconcerting, as well I might, but when I told the story around the village, everyone smiled and said, 'Oh yes, that's Claudia,' and in the end I met her again, and she stood and talked a bit and revealed that she was a great reader, and so we used to chat, now and then, if we met in the fields on those October days when it was getting cooler and mistier, and the smoke was coiling up from bonfires on the horizon and the shadows were turning mauve. I took her to be a County lady, who had had a good education, for she was formidably well read. Then one afternoon, when Jessica and I went looking for mushrooms and not finding any, she went by, with the dog and the gun, and said, 'Can't stop. Come to tea tomorrow, after milking.'

Come to tea? Where? After *milking*?

So I asked around again and they all smiled and said, 'Yes, that's Claudia! Cross Path Farm.'

So we went. At the end of the long, straight drive is a barred gate, with an elegant sign. 'Cross Path Farm. Accredited Champion Guernsey Herd. C.M.E. Hay.'

We closed the gate carefully behind us and drove on. We could see the farm and the farm buildings ahead, but because the land is completely flat down here, as flat as the Fen itself, and the driveway so straight and because there was that slight mist all around, it seemed to be much nearer than it actually was, and to recede from us as we drove. Odd.

The drive, the farmyard, the gravelled path in front of the house, and the buildings, the barn, the dairy, the milking parlour, all were so immaculate, so utterly clean and shining that they looked as if they had just been washed down. The hedges were trimmed, walls and gates unblemished. I have never seen such a model of neatness and order as Claudia's farm.

When I switched off the car engine, I heard the hiss of a hose, and the sound of machinery humming, and when we went to investigate, we found Claudia in the milking parlour, sluicing it down after the afternoon milking, which was just over. While she finished, we went and looked over a gate at the cows, their empty udders flaccid and soft beneath them, tails swishing against the flies. Beautiful animals. They looked as if they had been washed and groomed, too, their coats gleamed with good health. From this herd, the finest, richest milk goes out each day in large quantities, and I regretted the coming of rules and regulations which forbade us from taking our jug down and getting some of the creamy, warm flow straight from the cows. Farmers and their families can drink their own milk, but they are forbidden from passing it on to anyone else, whether for payment or not.

'Trick!' Claudia called, coming out, and the retriever appeared from nowhere and glued itself to her heel as we went towards the house. We had not brought Tinker.

'Come in.'

It is a long, low farmhouse, with one room leading out of the next all the way along, and wide windowsills. The front faces the sloping fields that rise up towards Barley, the back overlooks the farm buildings and the Fen. The whole place is comfortable, in a deep, soft, chintz-covered armchair and sporting-print sort of way. There are a few valuable antique pieces of furniture – a grandfather clock, with a moon painted on its face, a secretaire, a corner cupboard, and a dresser full of Worcester and Spode.

The two other things I noticed that first day were the cases and cases of books, and the rows and rows of framed certificates, trophies and shields, decorated about with rosettes, won by Claudia's champion cattle at shows up and down the country.

As we drank tea and ate bread and lemon curd and ginger cake in the kitchen, where there was not a thing out of place, not a speck of dust or dirt, I watched the Hon. Claudia, trying to work out what made her tick. She could be anywhere between thirty-five and fifty, though I guessed at forty-three. She is very tall, thin, pretty, in a bony, angular way, with well-cut hair and well-cut clothes. She could be a wealthy farmer's wife, a titled racehorse breeder, even a working Duchess. She lives absolutely alone though she has a couple in an adjacent cottage who look after the house and garden, and a stockman. She has only the dairy herd, no other animals, and a few acres of arable to supply some of her own cattle feed.

Claudia's father was an Earl and a lawyer, a barrister with a London practice and a house in the country. Her mother came from farming families in Scotland, and had a title in her own right. Claudia was their only child and, she told me, a clever one. She read law at Cambridge, though she was more interested in literature, but from her childhood, she had loved the country and wanted to work in it, and when she came down from University, she proceeded to apprentice herself to two farmers, one with sheep, and then a large-scale dairy-farmer in Devon. There she might have remained, on the lowest rung of the ladder, unless, as she put it, she had 'married upwards'. I got the impression she was not keen on the idea, but then came some family money, inherited from her mother's side, 'rather a lot', she looked about for the right farm, and began to build up her herd of Guernseys. From the start, she wanted to have the best and to be the best, to win every prize that was going. After fifteen years or so, she has done it.

She seems to have a large number of friends all over the country, and some family, whom she sees occasionally, but to have no one very close to her, man or woman, and not to need anyone either. She is pleasant, equable, a little clipped in manner, and she talks to children as she does to cows and dogs. In her spare time, she reads. She is as well and as widely read in English literature as many a don, she buys a lot of books, and when she goes to shows and markets with her Guernseys, she spends half her time in the ring and the other half in the local bookshops.

I felt, that first afternoon, exactly the same about Claudia as I still feel. I am a little afraid of her, though I also think that she is rather shy and conceals it behind her abrupt manner. What goes on, if anything, deep down inside her, whether she has any sadness or loneliness, any secret ambitions or emotions, or whether she is simply as she seems to be I cannot decide. There is no clue. I admire her greatly, though I do not envy her, and if I discovered one day that she had a secret life, or a skeleton in her cupboard, I shouldn't be surprised.

Meanwhile, we like to go and watch her do the milking, and to stroke the flanks of her placid, contented cows, and be amazed at the obedience of the dog Trick, and talk books with her. And wonder.

Creatures

I HAD some friends who went to live in a somewhat gloomy Jacobean mansion in an East Anglian village, where they stayed for four years, before leaving, rather abruptly, at the end of one autumn. Their next home was a first-floor flat in the heart of London. I was not surprised, for they were not country-lovers except, as it were, on paper. They knew nothing about country life, had no roots there, did not garden and could scarcely tell a sheep from a goat. They had thought it would be 'a good life for the children' but what in detail they really meant by this they could not say, and in any case the children were away at boarding school for much of the year. But what was it that finally drove them back to the city where they truly belonged? Was it the silence or the inconvenience of the countryside, the distance from friends and civilisation, the difficulty of getting proper help in the home and garden? No, they said, they had somehow become inured to all that. They might have stuck it out for longer, because they still somehow believed they ought to be enjoying their life in the country, still pretended it was doing them good, and anyway, dreaded the house-selling-and-buying and moving business heartily. But no, what finally drove them mad that last autumn were the creepy-crawlies. She went into their bathroom one September morning, lifted up her tooth-mug, and saw an enormous spider staring up at her from the bottom of it, started to scream and did not stop, in spirit at least, until they were driving away from their country house for the last time.

I can understand that. It is the autumn that brings them out, the dews and the coolness, night and morning, the general seasonal damp. I do not like creepy-crawlies but you simply have to get used to them, grin and bear them, keep a stiff-upper lip in a place like Moon Cottage, and unless you have a serious phobia, you do become less jittery about them all in time. It is the suddenness of spiders which is so unnerving, of course, their absolute silence and stealth, the way they are simply there under your hand or your bare foot, where the second before they certainly were not.

In the porch of Moon Cottage, there is a truly magnificent spider, living in a secret hole by day and emerging at night, to hang motionless in the centre of his complicated web, waiting to trap the flies that zoom in when we turn on the outside light. As it is frequently on, to light the steps for one of us coming home, or going to lock up the hens or fetch something from the garage or the shed, he does rather well, and we have a fine view of him. His body is an inch in diameter, and bears a pale, egg-like protrusion on its back, his legs are hairy and many-jointed, and if you dare to put a finger into his web, you see him palpate ever so slightly. I try to regard him dispassionately, to see him as handsome. I do not greatly mind him so long as he stays exactly where he is, but when he vanishes, I become agitated, for who is to know where he will pop up next?

We have spiders in the bathroom, in the washbasins, in the shower, and stalking about across the carpet, so many of them at this time of year that the cats become lazy about them, cannot be bothered to catch and chase them at all. Then, overnight, the weather turns very cold indeed, there is a sharp early morning frost and every spider has gone.

So have the wasps. The jam- and jelly- and chutney-making sessions of autumn bring them into the kitchen in droves. I become very expert indeed at killing them on the wing with the heel of my shoes, not for the joy of it, but because I am badly allergic to their sting. This year, we had to resort to a man with a nasty chemical to eradicate three nests of them in the crevices of the old stone walls.

I hope I would never kill a bee, but I wonder why I make such a distinction. Is it just because bees produce a food (one which I do not at all like), or because of their quite astonishing life-cycle and behaviour? Wasps are helpful in the garden, because they kill off a lot of pests, when feeding their grubs. No, we kill insects so casually, because the act does not fill us with the same misgiving, guilt and revulsion as would the slaughter of much larger animals or birds, and that, I think, is because they are so much smaller than we are, the act of killing them involves far less mess.

One evening in September, I went out to fetch something from the car, and heard a strange, shuffling, scuffling movement, among a pile of leaves that had blown into the back of the building. I did not investigate then, but the following evening, as Stanley came home, he picked up a hedgehog in his headlights, going smartly away across the path and into the ditch on the other side of the lane.

There have been several of them squashed on the country roads recently for they curl up into a ball and go still at the sound of an approaching vehicle, an almost inevitably fatal piece of behaviour.

I put down a saucer of milk for the garage hedgehog and every night it was taken. Then, at last, I saw him drinking it, noisily, greedily, before he turned away from the light of my torch and went off into the night.

Before the first hard frosts, we have to poke about in any piles of rubbish destined for the bonfire, for hedgehogs have a way of hibernating themselves there, and getting roasted on Guy Fawkes night or before. They are curiously appealing creatures, for all their fleas, and a good many ancient legends attach to them, as they do to owls. There is nothing like literary or mythical significance for provoking interest and affection for a particular wild creature. To have a house mouse or spider or even mole is tiresome, to have a party of roosting jackdaws in the chimney is worse, but to have our own hedgehog, by adoption, is very pleasing.

It was pleasing to see the pheasants still strutting about in the corn stubble and the meadows and on the edges of Lyke Wood, too, confident, handsome. A day or two later they were gone, taking shelter in the trees and hedgerows, and the fields were full of beaters and men with guns, and they were the confident ones, then, strutting about with their slavering dogs.

As the weather gets colder and the trees lose their leaves, the birds come back into the garden, the robin sings on the fence and the wren from the woodshed, and last week I saw the first bluetit for many a month. Down on the Fen, the summer visitors are leaving, or have already gone. There were a large number of warblers in the area this year, heard, though rarely seen, and certainly to me quite indistinguishable from one another. In June there were nightingales, though we did not manage to hear them. The bird population on the Fen changes constantly. At the end of autumn and in early winter, especially if it is wet – and it usually is – the ducks and geese will arrive there, and rest for a few days on their way north and east.

Down the lane from the church, on the telegraph wires, the swallows balance, I have never seen so many, the lane is noisy with their chattering and muttering all day long, and because the weather stayed so warm for so long, the birds lingered with the sunshine, and the late broods of young grew large and strong enough to undertake their migratory journey. Swallows and house-martins take longer over their assembling than the swifts, which wheel and scream about for a day or two and then are gone. When the wires are finally bare of those graceful, fork-tailed birds, it will seem suddenly quiet in the land, and colder, it will be almost winter.

When I lie in bed reading at night with the lamp on and the window open, the bedroom is alive with the pattering and battering and flapping of moths, and the crazy flying of the daddy-long-legs, too, and the buzz of small, winged, night insects I cannot identify, and occasionally, too, on a warm, damp September evening, a mosquito whines in, like one of those remote-controlled aeroplanes, around my head, until I am forced to leave my book and get up and get rid of them all, close the window.

The ledges the next morning are littered with a mess of wings and broken bodies, webs, and still-buzzing flies.

The whole year, in and around Moon Cottage, has been full of creatures which interweave with our own daily lives, the domestic animals, the hens, the garden birds, and the foxes and mice and hedgehogs and moles of the fields and woods beyond us, the farm animals all around and beyond us. Sometimes the sight or sound of a rare bird causes a stir but there has been nothing here that anyone might not see in any country village, or indeed in the town, for so many creatures encroach upon suburban gardens and waste land, and playing fields. Nothing, that is, until I went out just after sunset one evening in late September. I had been pruning back some of the thick rose-suckers near the tumbledown stone wall that separates Moon Cottage from the wilderness garden of the deserted house next door, and left the secateurs behind. It wouldn't rain tonight, but there would be the usual heavy dew of an autumn night, and secateurs rust in no time.

As I picked them up, I paused. From the garden over the wall, in the middle, where there are the old apple trees, I heard noises. It was too late for small boys to be scrumping, and besides, there were no voices, and boys cannot restrain themselves from chatting to each other as they climb. I waited. The sun was dropping lower in the sky and the long shadows lay over the grass and nettles. The noise again. The wilderness garden dips in the centre, and then slopes down, and the apple trees lean over this slope. They had been thick and red and leaning with fruit, and there are plum trees, too, though they have been sparsely fruited. I called to the dog, and went over to investigate. If a fox was on the prowl I wanted rid of him.

Down the lane, and through the gate set into the old high wall and almost off its hinges, tied up with bits of string. Tinker stopped dead, his ears pricked. Then he growled. And lay down at my feet.

It was dark now, the sun had dropped behind Lyke Wood in a great poppy-coloured ball and left behind a damson sky. We waited. Nothing. No one. If it was a fox, he was standing somewhere in the undergrowth, motionless. Then, a dozen yards away, under the apple tree, I saw him. He had come out of the long grass, up the slope from the hedge and ditch at the far end of the rambling garden which abuts on to the meadow, and he was feeding on windfall apples that lay all around. Not a fox at all. A badger. We must have been well out of his scent, and he cannot have been bothered by whatever he heard of our arrival, either. We had not made much sound, but badgers are usually extremely wary and shy.

Perhaps he was very hungry, perhaps he lived near enough to the fringe of human activity to be less guarded. But he stayed there, feeding, until it grew too dark for me to see him any longer – I had brought no lamp and there was only a thin moon.

From the grass and the trees around came a cool, sweet, damp smell of slow decay and fallen leaves and rotting fruit, mist, earth. The dog and I slipped away as quietly as we could, through the gate and out into the lane again.

Lately, there have been signs of activity at the deserted cottage, men looking expertly at roof and walls, surveyors, I suppose, and people trying to see in through the windows of the cottage, and then people inside it peering out at the garden speculatively. So it is to be sold, probably, restored and inhabited. I dread that, though that is extremely selfish. I dread what someone insensitive may do in rebuilding the place, and dread the smartening and tidying of the garden, for then no badgers, or owls, or nightjars or parties of long-tailed tits will come so close to us, the creatures will retreat further back, on to the Fen again. I shall not see a badger feeding off the windfall apples next autumn.

It is the first Sunday in October, it is Harvest Festival. And, because last Wednesday was Michaelmas Day, we are celebrating that in retrospect, at the same time, with a fine, fat goose for lunch, collected yesterday from Cuckoo Farm.

As we walk up the lane to the church, the mist is still thick, and raw, the air chilly. The holly bushes and gravestones loom out from it around the churchyard.

Inside, it is wonderful, it is the day to crown all the year, golden and glorious, rich and ripe, to see and to smell, the old church looks best of all when decorated in this sort of abundant way. Here are pumpkins, like suns shining from the windowledges, and a marrow the size of a barrage balloon, leaning against the font. Here are strings of onions hanging from the pulpit and tomatoes and apples and pears and plums piled up in baskets and spilling over on to the steps. Michaelmas daisies and chrysanthemums are everywhere. Up beside the altar is a table set with jars of preserves, blackberry and damson, apple and raspberry and strawberry, jars of marmalade and buttery lemon curd and dark, dark chutney. Here are dozens of eggs in a mixing bowl, and cobnuts and walnuts and hazelnuts in baskets, and mushrooms picked that morning in the fields where Lavender's horses graze. The children have made friezes and painted pictures and stuck collages, and hung them all down one side of the church, showing the leaves and berries of autumn and the work of the farmers in the fields and of the gardeners in the gardens, and the animals gathering their stores against the winter. Here is a sheaf of corn, and there a bale of hay, and a wonderful loaf of bread, all pleated and plaited, standing beside the chalice.

The church is four times as full as it ever is except on Christmas and Easter Days, for people in the city come out to villages at Harvest Festival time, to savour the atmosphere and see the fruits of the earth and sing the familiar thanksgiving hymns.

The farmers we have been seeing in open-necked shirts and old straw hats, on tractors and wagons and combines, are here in best suits with stiff collars and newly-shaven, sunburned faces, and the gardeners are out of their old boots and muddy corduroys and into clean linen.

It is, I suppose, an unrealistic, rather dated service, and I wonder whether it is not smug to give thanks for the harvest when so much of the world is empty-bellied and so much of what *our* world produces is stored in mountains and so-called surpluses, the fruits from orchards and fields are wickedly wasted, left to rot or ploughed back into the ground or dumped in pits and buried. How can we hurl the gifts of God back in his face in that way, how *dare* we squander and waste, or else clutch greedily to ourselves for more money, more money, when little children and old men and women are dying of hunger and poverty?

The words of the hymns ought to burn us through, the feasting turn to ashes in our mouths.

And yet . . . these *are* the fruits of the earth around us, these are the people who have laboured to grow them and gather them in, and we shall eat well and be warm in our beds, through the coming winter, we have enough to share. There are some services of the church which seem to me to be perfect expressions of certain truths that do not change, and could not be improved upon by being changed themselves, but which *can* bear all the weight of new meaning, in new times, as well as repetition of the old.

The produce in the church is collected up in boxes and taken to the elderly and the needy in city parishes, and in addition there are gifts of tinned goods, and cakes and bread, which are collected in the church hall.

When we go out of the cool church, it is into bright, mellow sunshine, warm, but not hot, and we look over the rooftop towards the Fen, and the hills beyond. We see ploughed fields and trees tinged ochre and rust-red, an autumn countryside.

I feel satisfied, glad the garden has done so well, glad there has been such an excellent grain harvest, with week after week of sunshine to ripen the corn and make its gathering-in so easy for the farmers, glad that we are going down the lane to Moon Cottage, where the apples are ripe on the tree and the pantry is packed with preserves, where the goose sizzles richly in the oven and the sunflowers are high as the house, and have shining faces.

We are all here, my family, the animals, all safe, all well and happy and free in the sunshine, and up the lane and down the lane, the houses of friends and neighbours, and beyond our low stone wall, the 'happy autumn fields'. The countryside is at its best, mellow, ripe, glorious. It is a time for rejoicing, it is easy to be glad here, to praise, to be thankful. We have had the best of years.

I go to the top of the seven stone steps and look down, at the magic apple tree and at my daughter dancing beneath it, arms outspread to the cats and the dog, and to the bending sunflowers and the country beyond, the Buttercup field, the Rise, and all the flat Fen, still sunlit, all the sky, still blue.

And then, I remember again the words of Thomas Traherne:

I seemed as one brought into the estate of innocence. All things were spotless and pure and glorious, yea and infinitely mine and joyful and precious. I knew not that there were any sins or complaints or laws. I dreamed not of poverties, contentions or vices. All tears and quarrels were hidden from mine eyes. Everything was at rest, free and immortal. I knew nothing of sickness or death or exaction, in the absence of these I was entertained like an angel with the works of God in their splendour and glory. I saw all in the peace of Eden. Heaven and earth did sing my creator's praises and could not make more melody to Adam than to me. All time was eternity and a perpetual Sabbath. Is it not strange that an infant should be heir of the world and see those mysteries which the books of the learned never unfold?

A week later, the wind rose and tossed the branches of the magic apple tree and all the trees of Lyke Wood and Cuckoo Spinney and the sycamores in the field leading to the orchard garden and the hazels that bound it and the elms where the rooks roost and the great walnut tree beside Albert Baker's cottage, so that the air was full of leaves spinning and whirling and the ground thick with leaves fallen. The sky was grey, and heavy with clouds, racing, piling up one on top of the other, darkening over the Fen. Rain came, first on the wind, in soft clouds, then in a downpour soaking the earth, mulching all the leaves to a mould. The clocks came forward, the days were suddenly short and the nights long, lights came on, and we could see them again through the trees, the village of Barley drew closer in upon itself again, for warmth and comfort and companionship.

I went out to the woodshed to bring in the first armful of logs and a bunch of kindling. And looked over my shoulder, across the darkening garden, to the house. The lamps were on, and shining out to me.

I picked up my log basket and went towards the cottage and, as I did so, the wind gusted off the Fen towards the apple tree, taking the last of the leaves, the last remaining apples, and leaving the branches bare.

I shivered. The year had turned again. It was winter.

I went inside quickly, and closed the door.